KNOWLEDGE ENCYCLOPEDIA
HUMAN BODY
LUNGS & RESPIRATORY SYSTEM

© Wonder House Books 2024

All rights reserved. No part of this book may be reproduced or transmitted in any form by any means, electronic or mechanical, including photocopying and recording, or by any information storage and retrieval system except as may be expressly permitted in writing by the publisher.

(An imprint of Prakash Books)

contact@wonderhousebooks.com

Disclaimer: The information contained in this encyclopedia has been collated with inputs from subject experts. All information contained herein is true to the best of the Publisher's knowledge.

ISBN : 9789389931211

Table of Contents

The Breath of Life	3
Nose: Your Breath's Gatekeeper	4–5
Taking Air to the Lungs	6–7
The Last Mile: Bronchi and Bronchioles	8
Destination: Lungs	9
Inside Your Lungs	10–11
The Respiratory Cycle	12
Taking Oxygen to the Tissues	13
Oxygen and Carbon Dioxide Cycles	14–15
Cellular Respiration	16
Breathing Underwater	17
Breathing at High Altitudes	18
Asthma	19
Poison in the Air	20–21
Under the Weather	22–23
Invaders of Your Lungs	24–25
Exercises to Breathe Better	26
Your Body's Sound Box	27
Making Words, Making Sense	28–29
Fluid in Your Lungs	30
Bringing Someone Back to Life	31
Word Check	32

THE BREATH OF LIFE

As long as we are breathing, we are alive. Life starts with a baby's first breath when it comes into the world. The shock of life wakes babies up as air rushes in through the nose, past the windpipe and into the lungs. From then onwards, the lungs work without rest, to filter oxygen from the air and pass it into the circulatory system. Here, oxygen is pumped by the heart and taken to every cell of the body. The waste, carbon dioxide, is taken to the lungs where it is forced out of the body by the contraction of the lungs.

But what if there is a problem? If the tissues sense a lack of oxygen, they send a signal to the brain, which then makes the lungs work harder. The intercostal muscles of the ribcage then pull together, shrinking and expanding the lungs harder to push out stale air and pull in fresh air. The nose and the sinuses work day and night to filter germs from the air before letting it into the body. The pharynx works to separate air from food, making sure you do not choke and also making sure no air enters your stomach—so you do not feel bloated. In between all of these processes, the larynx works quietly to make the sounds that make a language. Perhaps it is working right now, as you read this book out loud.

The day the system stops, because of a weak heart that cannot pump any more, or weak or polluted lungs that cannot breathe in fresh air any more, one dies.

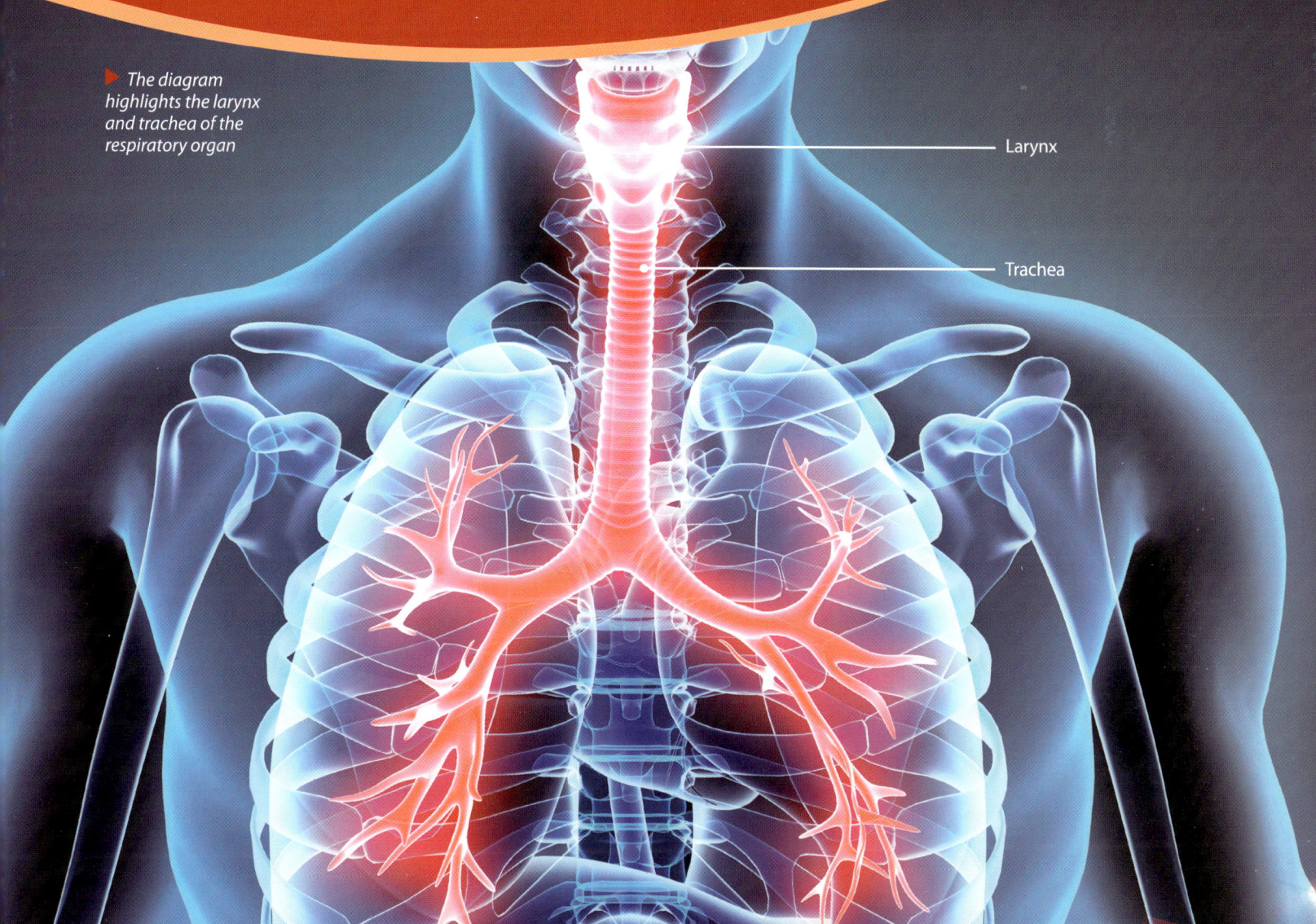

▶ *The diagram highlights the larynx and trachea of the respiratory organ*

Larynx

Trachea

Nose: Your Breath's Gatekeeper

Most of the respiratory system is made up of the vessels that bring fresh air right into the body. First there is the **conducting zone** which includes the nose, throat, windpipe and air passages inside the lungs. The **respiratory zone** consists of the tissue where oxygen filters from the lungs into the blood.

The nose is the gateway of the conducting zone. There is more to it than the part that sticks out of your face, as it occupies a large space inside your head, between the brain and the mouth. It cleans the air that comes in through the nostrils, removing dust and germs. That is why you normally breathe through your nose, else air enters the lungs from the mouth.

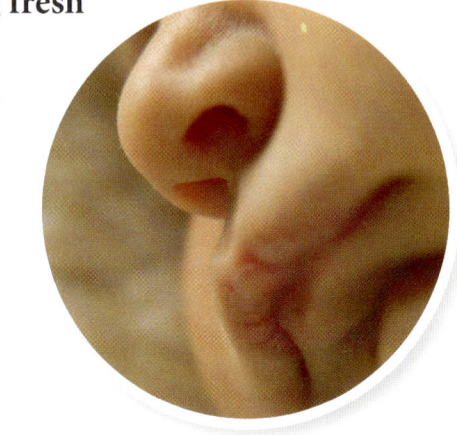

▲ When you are stressed out, inhaling and exhaling makes you feel better

Outer Nose

The part of the nose that you can touch and see is called the bridge of the nose. It is made of a cartilage septum and thickened skin that make the nostrils on either side. The inside of your nostrils is like the outer skin with sebum glands and hair. This hair keeps big dust particles, dirt and even insects from entering the nose. Interestingly, human beings mostly breathe through one nostril at a time, even though we have two nostrils. If you want to check this fact, put your hands close to your nose and breathe in, then breathe out.

In Real Life

Some germs, like the flu virus, can infect your sinus. Your body's immune response causes them to swell. You can feel them on your face. This swelling causes facial pain, headache and sometimes, fever. It often follows a cold, leaving you with a runny nose.

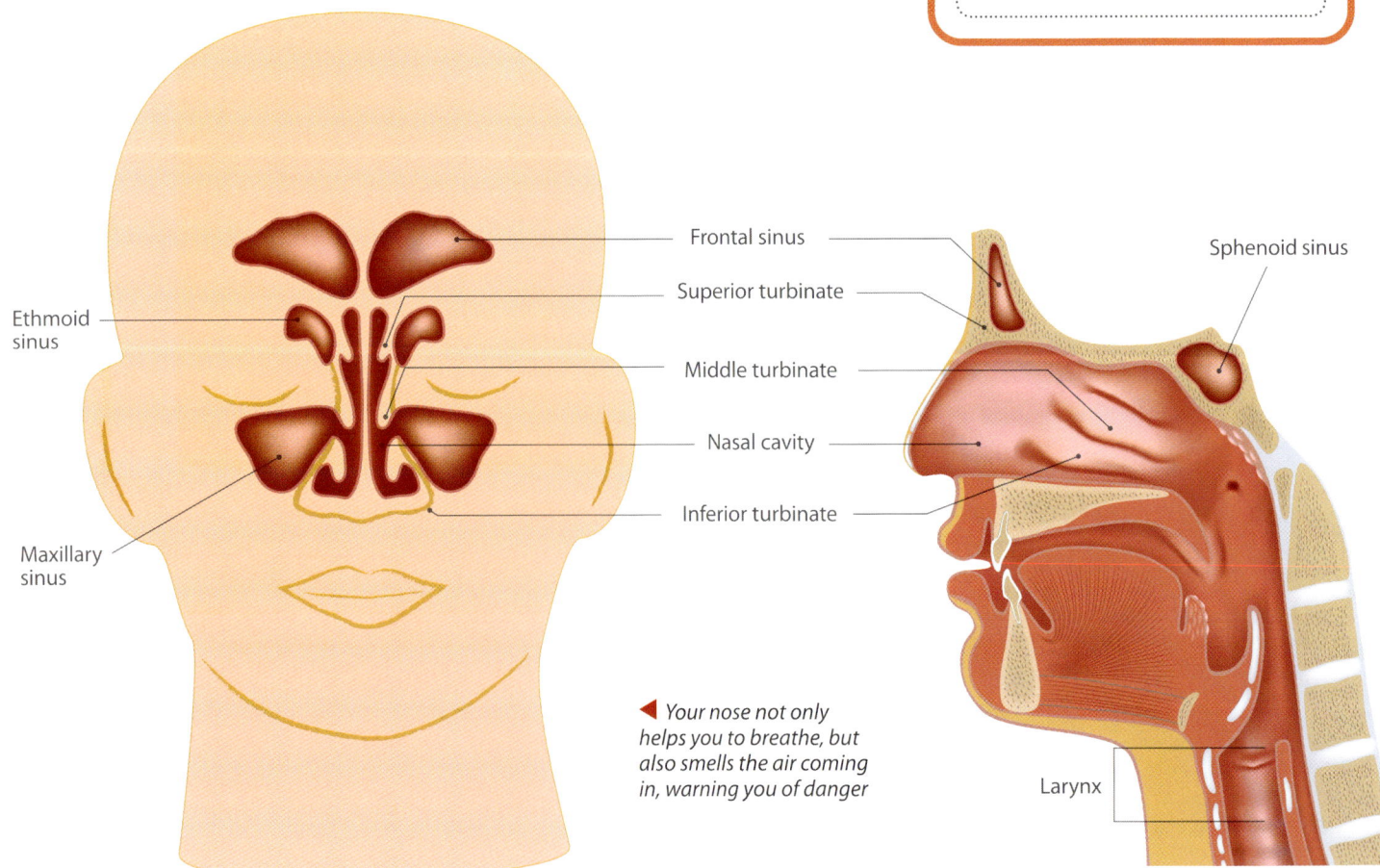

◄ Your nose not only helps you to breathe, but also smells the air coming in, warning you of danger

Inside the Nose

The septum extends right through the inner nose, where it is made of bone. It is not always in the centre, but often slightly shifted to the right or left. The bony walls of the nose are folded into **conchae** or turbinates. They swirl the air within the nose, like turbines in a generator. When you are breathing out, the nasal conchae trap water vapour so your nose does not become dry. The inner nose also has extensions called **paranasal sinuses**, of which there are four pairs—the frontal, maxillary, sphenoidal and ethmoidal. The air in them makes the skull light.

Incredible Individuals

Cleopatra, the Queen of Egypt, had a long nose. Blaise Pascal once famously remarked, that had Cleopatra's nose been shorter, the whole face of the world would have been changed. He was referring rhetorically to the collapse of the Roman republic, as both, Julius Caesar and Marc Antony were spellbound by her beauty.

▲ A bust of Cleopatra

Sneezing

Sneezing is our body's way of keeping itself healthy by expelling germs, pollen and other foreign objects with great force. The hair in your nostril are sensitive to the smallest things and trigger the nervous system to make the muscles of the chest and throat contract very fast. When you sneeze, air is forced out of your mouth and nose together. As the air moves out, it carries mucus droplets with it, in which the germs are trapped. If somebody happens to be near you when you sneeze, they might inhale your germs. That is why you should cover your nose and mouth while sneezing.

Cleaning the Air

The nose works like your body's own air purifier. The nasal cavity and sinuses are lined with a special **respiratory epithelium**. This is made of cells that have microscopic hair called cilia. Scattered in between are **goblet cells** that make mucus. As the air you breathe in swirls, the cilia and mucus catch all the dust and germs in it. Under the epithelium is a special tissue called **nasal-associated lymphoid tissue** (NALT), which has immune cells in it. These destroy the germs caught by the cilia. The mucus makes the air humid, while blood capillaries under the epithelium warm the air before it goes into the lungs. The 'purified air' is now ready for the lungs.

Isn't It Amazing!

Birds do not have external noses. Instead, they have a pair of openings called nares just above their beaks that open directly into their inner noses. The nares can be used to tell male from female. Budgerigar males have blue ones, while females have brown ones.

▲ Observe the nares on the bird's beak

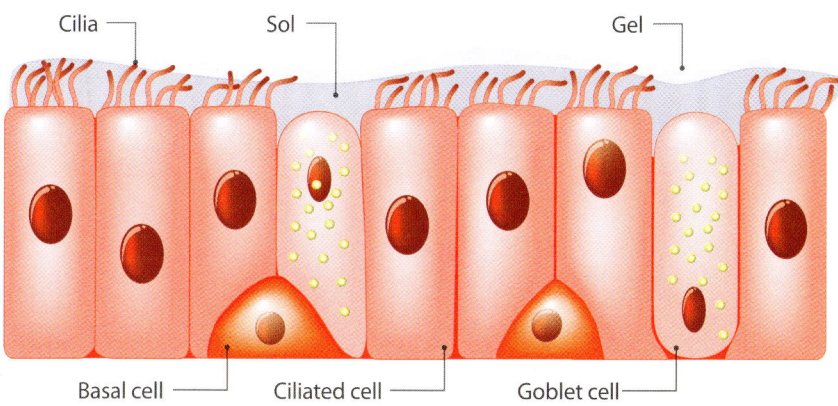

▲ The nasal mucus is made of a sticky, outer gel that traps germs and a fluid inner sol that moves it

Taking Air to the Lungs

Once air is cleaned and conditioned in the nose, it passes into the pharynx. This acts like a railway junction, where two tracks meet. The digestive system brings food from the mouth to the food pipe. The respiratory system brings air to the windpipe. So why do they meet at all?

If these two 'tracks' did not meet, we would not be able to speak at all *(see pp 27–29)*. During an emergency, when more air has to be sucked in or forced out, you breathe from the mouth. The flipside is that it creates the danger of choking, if food entered the windpipe. There is one simple way to prevent it—do not talk while eating!

▲ *You should avoid talking while eating because the food might accidentally enter your trachea and interrupt your breathing*

Parts of the Pharynx

The pharynx is made of muscle that helps you inhale air and also swallow food. It is made of three parts—the **nasopharynx**, the **oropharynx** and the **laryngopharynx**. The nasopharynx is the extension of the inner nose to the throat. It has the **pharyngeal tonsils**, also called the adenoids, which hang down from the top like a fold of tissue. These are full of immune cells that kill any germs that have made it past the nose. It has another flap of tissue called the **uvula** that extends from the palate, which separates the nose from the mouth. While swallowing, the uvula stops food from entering the nose. The nasopharynx also has two canals called eustachian tubes that connect it to the ears so that they can be of the same pressure as the atmosphere, or else the ear drums will burst.

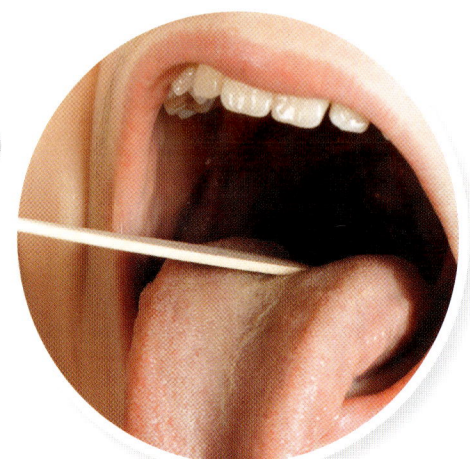

▲ *A patient's tonsils being checked by a doctor*

The oropharynx is the middle part, where the two tracks cross. The hyoid bone and the spinal column surround it. The hyoid attaches two sets of muscles. The first is the tongue inside the mouth. Under the tongue are the **lingual tonsils**. The other set are the muscles that control the **epiglottis**. The epiglottis shuts off the wind pipe while you swallow food. At the end of the palate, are the **palatine tonsils**. The final part is the laryngopharynx which leads the air into the trachea.

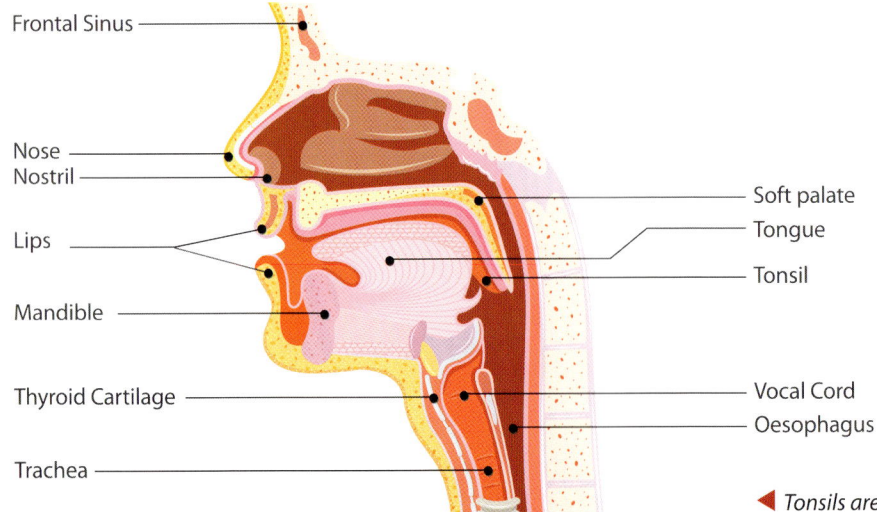

◀ *Tonsils are large in children but shrink as they grow older*

In Real Life

Infections acquired during childhood may leave you with enlarged tonsils. These cause obstructions to breathing that might need to be removed by surgery. If not, they can cause snoring or breathlessness.

Trachea

The trachea (wind pipe) takes air from the pharynx to the lungs, sharing space in the neck with the oesophagus (food pipe). It is ringed by 20 C-shaped pieces of cartilage that make sure that it does not collapse onto itself like the oesophagus does. The **trachealis muscle** attaches to these pieces and, along with other tissues, makes the main air tube. It helps to stretch the trachea when breathing out, and shrink it when breathing in. In the lungs, the trachea branches into **bronchi**.

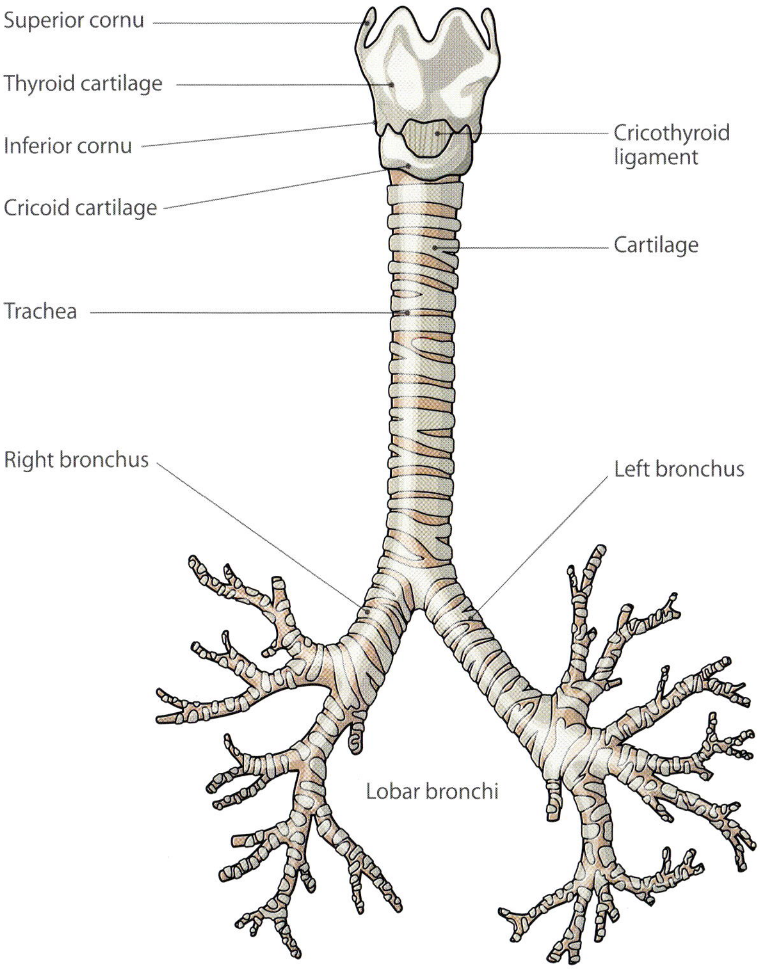

- Superior cornu
- Thyroid cartilage
- Inferior cornu
- Cricoid cartilage
- Trachea
- Right bronchus
- Cricothyroid ligament
- Cartilage
- Left bronchus
- Lobar bronchi

▲ The tracheal epithelium also has cilia, which brush germs towards the nose, so they can be sneezed out

💡 Isn't It Amazing!

A giraffe's long neck also means they have really long pharynxes and tracheas. Their lung muscles have to work a lot to inhale and exhale air. The air passing through the trachea does not have enough force to vibrate the vocal cords, so giraffes are mostly silent animals.

▶ A giraffe's wind pipes take air down or up over 6 feet, which is a really long way

▶ You might sneeze because you are exposed to dust particles, so keep your surroundings clean

The Last Mile: Bronchi and Bronchioles

When the trachea reaches a point in the chest just below the neck, called carina, it splits into two bronchi (singular: bronchus) to the left and right. The carina has nerves that can sense whether anything other than air has fallen down the trachea. If there is, it will trigger coughing. Muscles in the trachea will try to push the body out before it enters the lungs. Otherwise, it may cause you to faint or cause your breathing to stop. (*see pp 26*)

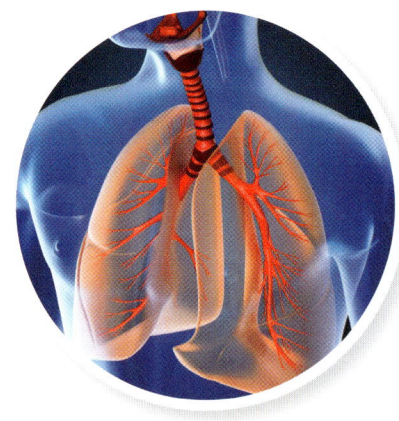

▲ *The bronchi and bronchioles make the bronchial tree*

The bronchi enter the lungs, where they further split into secondary and tertiary branches. All of these have cartilage rings to stop them from collapsing. Doctors call the point of entry the **hilum**, where the nerves, pulmonary arteries and lymph vessels also enter and the pulmonary vein leaves.

Isn't It Amazing!

Insects have a very different respiratory system. They have tiny pores under the bodies called spiracles, which let air into large sacs. Tubes called trachea take air around the body, branching into tiny tracheoles, which deliver oxygen to cells.

▶ *Unlike vertebrates, an insect's respiratory and circulatory systems do not interact*

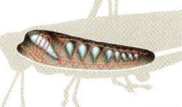

Bronchioles

Bronchioles branch off from tertiary bronchi and branch off, in turn, to form terminal bronchioles. These feed the units of gas exchange in the lungs called **alveoli**. They have no cartilage.

Cross-section

The bronchioles are lined inside by epithelial tissue which has cilia to brush germs and dust out of the lungs, and also goblet cells that make mucus to help them. Surrounding it is a piece of loose tissue called the **lamina propria**. Like the nose has NALT, the lamina propria has BALT or **bronchial-associated lymphatic tissue**. It has immune cells in it, which destroy germs. This is surrounded by smooth muscle that keeps the air moving.

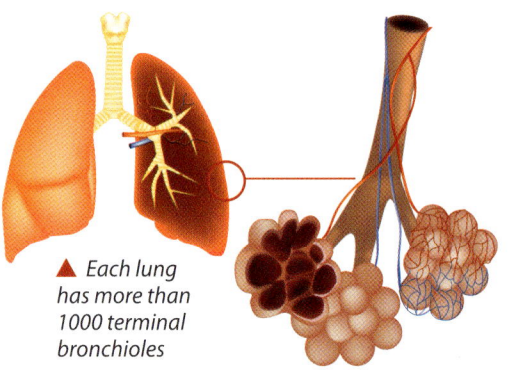

▲ *Each lung has more than 1000 terminal bronchioles*

In Real Life

Infection in the bronchioles leads to a build-up of mucus, which causes congested lungs. This is called **bronchitis**.

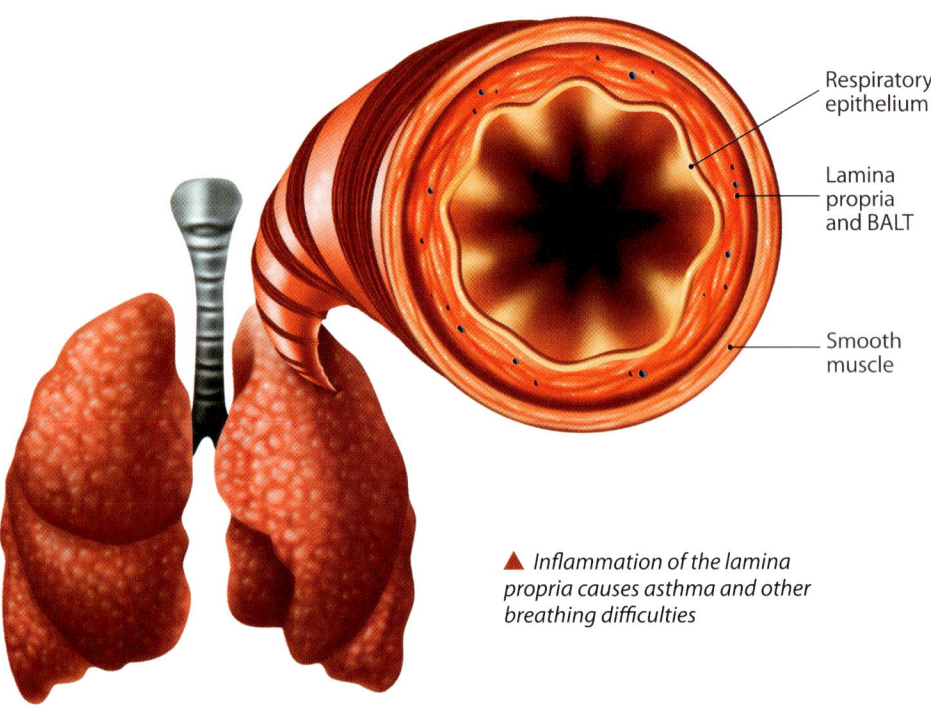

▲ *Inflammation of the lamina propria causes asthma and other breathing difficulties*

Destination: Lungs

The air you take in from your nose has to reach the respiratory zone. Here, the respiratory system meets the circulation system. This zone has two parts, the **respiratory bronchioles** and the **pulmonary lobes**. It is made up of special tissue which allows oxygen to diffuse right into blood, where haemoglobin in the red blood cells is waiting for it. The blood has let go of carbon dioxide from deep within your body's tissues. It is now ready to make the journey to the outside world. Thus, you complete one breath.

Lung Structure

Your lungs come in a pair, with the left lung slightly smaller than the right one. Both lungs are encased in the ribcage and covered by a bag called the **pleura** (plural: pleurae), which cushions them against the ribs. The **diaphragm**, a giant, dome-shaped muscle, seals off the ribcage from below. The left lung has the cardiac notch, a space it makes for the heart to fit in.

Each lung is made up of lobes, which are served by secondary bronchi. The larger, right lung has three lobes, while the left lung has just two. Each lobe is divided into segments, which are then divided into lobules, each of which gets a bronchiole. Lobules are divided into alveolar sacs that, in turn, have alveoli within them. The alveoli are the functional units of the lungs.

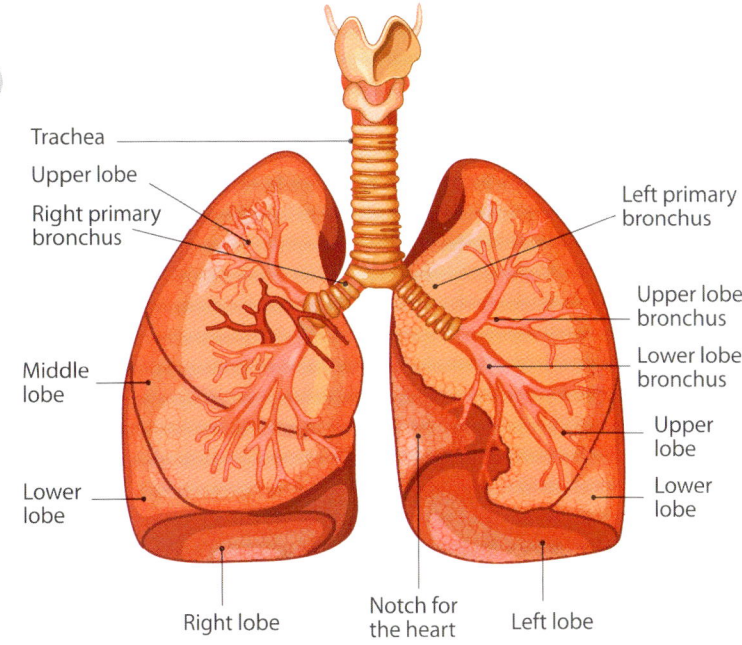

▲ *The right lung is broader than the left lung*

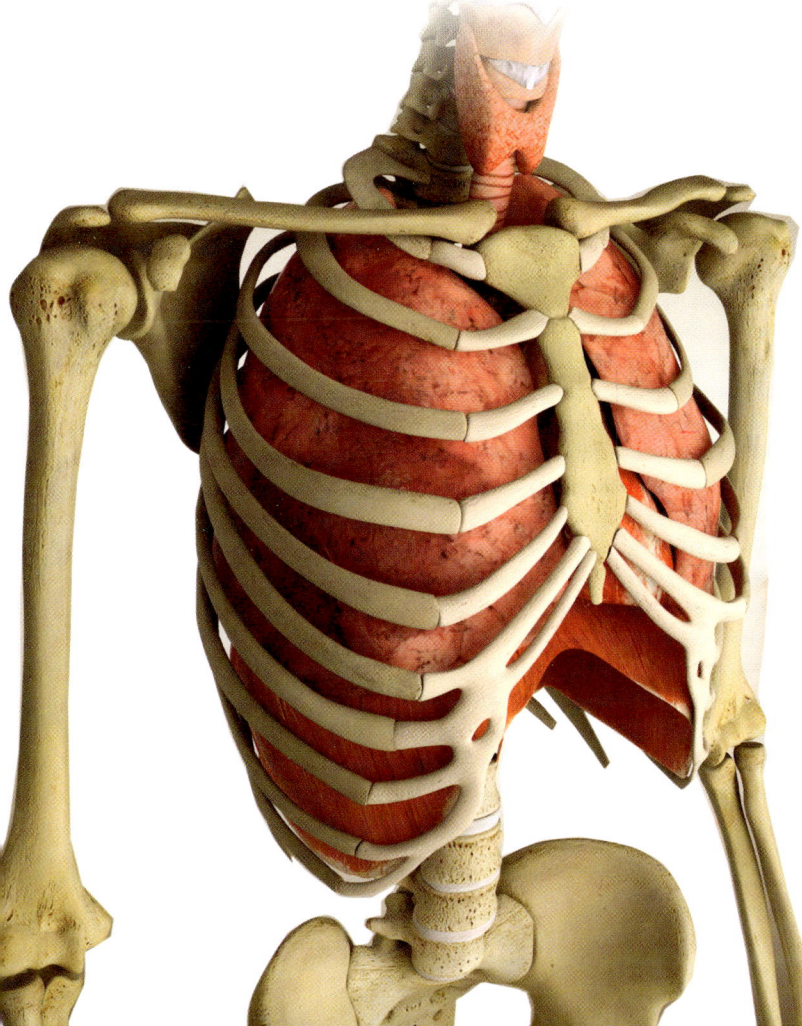

Pleurae

The pleurae that cover your lungs are made of two layers. The inner layer (visceral pleura) lines your lungs directly, while the outer layer (parietal pleura) links them to the rib cage, sternum and diaphragm. Between them is the pleural cavity, which is full of air. Pleurae act like a cushion, when the inflated lungs push against the rib cage. They also protect the lungs against infections. The pleurae may swell up due to infection, leading to a condition called pleurisy. It may cause dry cough and difficulty in breathing. Sometimes, the pleural cavity may be filled with too much air, pushing pressure on the lungs. This is called pneumothorax. Injury to the lungs may cause them to be filled with blood, leading to a condition called haemothorax.

◀ *The pleural sac cushions the lungs while breathing*

Inside Your Lungs

In many invertebrate organisms, the respiratory system does not interact with the circulatory system. It starts doing so in molluscs, where **haemocyanin** molecules in the haemolymph (they have no blood) receive oxygen from the gills. Red blood cells develop in fishes to carry oxygenated blood from the gills to the heart, then through the body and bring back deoxygenated blood to the gills again. In reptiles, birds and mammals, the lungs take over. There separate arteries for oxygenated blood and veins for deoxygenated blood develop. This brings a lot more oxygen to the tissues, so they can have a lot more energy.

Blood Vessels and Nerves

Lungs are the only organs that receive deoxygenated blood from the heart's **pulmonary arteries**, which come straight to them from the heart's right ventricle. The artery enters at the hilum and follows the **bronchial tree**, branching into arterioles as it branches. At the alveoli, the blood flows in tiny capillaries, ready to receive oxygen. They collect into venules, which follow the bronchial tree till the hilum, where the **pulmonary vein** leaves to enter the heart's left atrium.

The lungs are controlled by the parasympathetic and sympathetic nervous systems. The parasympathetic ('rest and digest') system constricts the bronchial tree, causing deeper breathing, like when you are sleeping. The sympathetic ('fight or flight') nervous system dilates the bronchial tree, so you have more oxygenation.

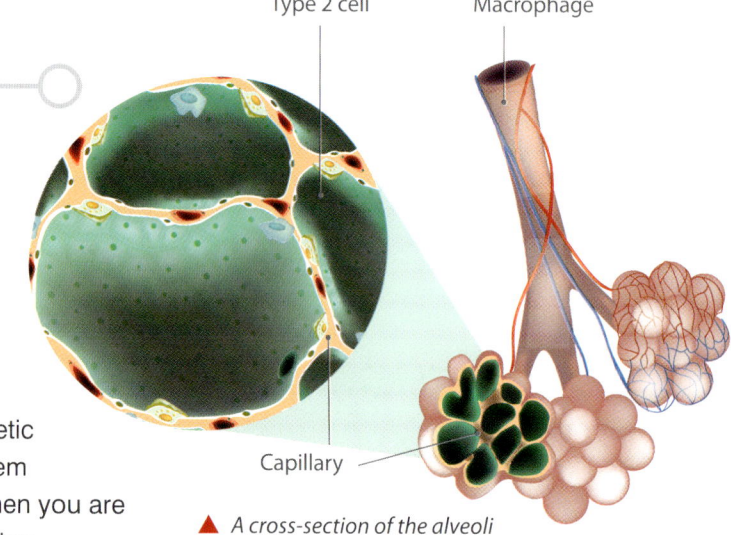

▲ A cross-section of the alveoli showing walls and capillaries

In Real Life

The corneas of your eyes get oxygen from the air. This eventually dissolves into tears.

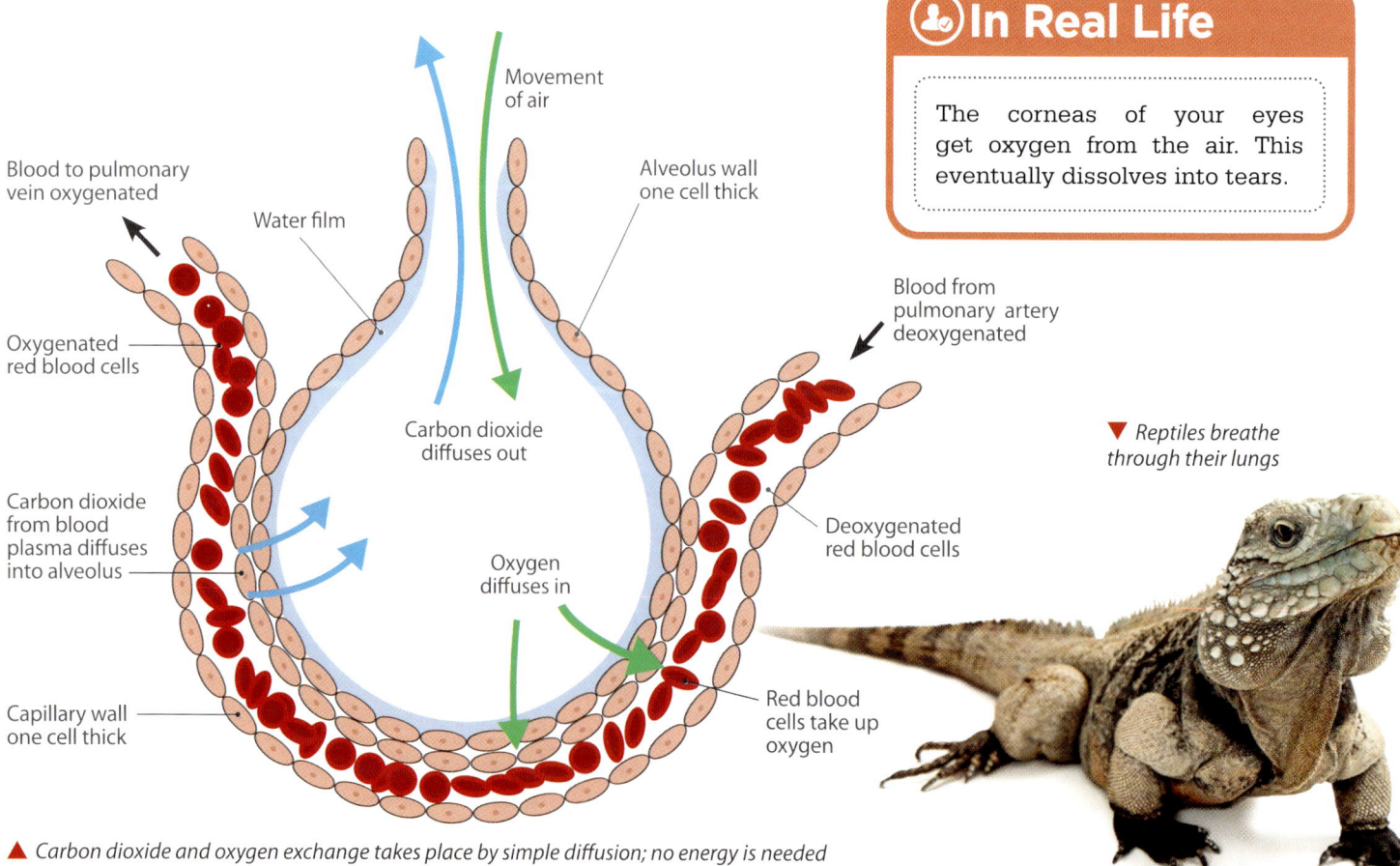

▲ Carbon dioxide and oxygen exchange takes place by simple diffusion; no energy is needed

▼ Reptiles breathe through their lungs

HUMAN BODY | LUNGS & RESPIRATORY SYSTEM | 11

Alveoli

These are the working parts of the lungs and look like a bunch of grapes under a microscope. Each alveolus is a sack of respiratory cells, just 0.2 mm thick, with walls that stretch when full of air. They link to each other by alveolar pores, which make the air pressure in them equal. Most of the wall is made of type I alveolar cells, which let oxygen in and let carbon dioxide out. A few cells belong to the type II alveolar cell group, which make **pulmonary surfactant**. This is a soap-like substance that makes it easier for oxygen to dissolve in the water of plasma. Immune cells called **alveolar macrophages** roam around the alveoli, snapping up any germs that manage to get there.

Isn't It Amazing!

Mammals have tiny alveoli that are densely packed into their lungs, to increase surface area. For example, while a frog's alveolus is 10 times as wide, it has only 20 cm^2 of gas exchange area per cc (50.8 square inches per cubic inch), while human beings pack in 300 cm^2 of gas exchange area per cc (762 square inches per cubic inch).

▲ Frogs do most of their breathing through their skin

▼ Dolphins are mammals, not fish. They need to come up for air from time to time

Alveolar Pressure

During quiet breathing, the air pressure in your alveoli (**alveolar pressure**) will match atmospheric pressure, which is 760 mm Hg at sea level. However, it changes with the phase of breathing. When you are inhaling, your lungs expand and air pressure in your alveoli drops. Atmospheric air rushes in to make up the difference. When exhaling, the lungs contract and the alveoli get squeezed. Air pressure rises, and air rushes out to bring down the pressure. This is because of **Boyle's Law**, which says that the pressure and volume of a gas are inversely related.

The Respiratory Cycle

Your doctor's term for breathing is pulmonary ventilation (PV) or a respiratory cycle. One PV has two steps—breathing in or inspiration and breathing out or expiration. Inhalation is the term for when you deliberately breathe something in, like the air above food that smells delicious. Exhalation is for breathing out. Most of the time, you breathe quietly. This is called **eupnea**. When you are tired or doing something that needs more breath—like singing—your body switches to forced breathing. This is called **hyperpnea**.

▲ Singers need to control their breathing to carry a tune properly

You use two sets of muscles to breathe. The muscles between your ribs are called **intercostal muscles**. The diaphragm is the large muscle stretching between the ribs, sternum and lumbar vertebra.

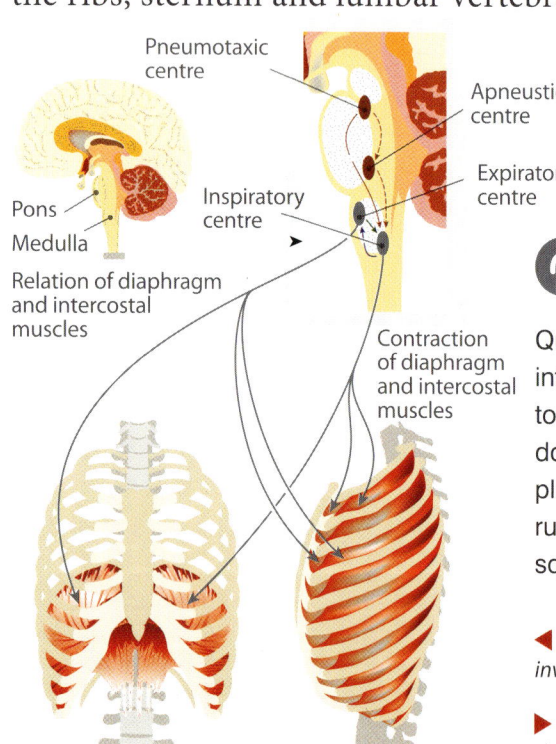

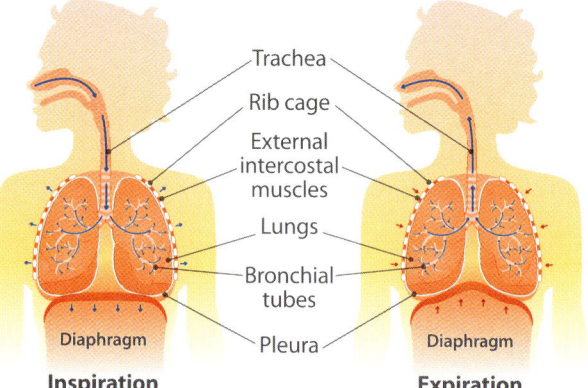

▶ Respiration works by using Boyle's Law of gas pressures

Quiet Breathing

Quiet breathing may be shallow or deep. In the shallow kind, only the intercostals contract and expand. Deep breathing involves the diaphragm too. During inspiration, the diaphragm contracts and pulls the pleurae down. The intercostals contract and pull the ribcage and the attached pleurae, upward and outward. Together, they expand the lung and air rushes in to equalise the alveolar pressure. When the muscles relax, they squeeze the pleurae, which then squeeze the lungs, forcing air out.

◀ In quiet breathing, your skeletal muscles work like involuntary muscles, controlled by the brain stem

▶ Forced breathing helps get rid of the lactic acid built up by the muscles during exercise in the form of CO_2, by oxidation

Forced Breathing

Other muscles join in when you need to breathe in or breathe out more air. This happens when your body needs more oxygen, like when you are tired after exercise or heavy work, or if you experience shortness of breath, or if you have asthma.

When breathing in, the neck muscles pull the ribcage upward, enlarging the chest beyond what the intercostals and diaphragm can do. Put your fingers on the base of your neck and breathe in deeply. Can you feel your shoulders rise?

When breathing out, the muscles of your belly, like the obliques, contract. This squeezes your belly, and the organs in it push the diaphragm up in turn. Pull in your stomach, and you can feel air rushing out of your nose.

Taking Oxygen to the Tissues

Oxygen diffuses from the alveoli into the pulmonary capillaries under atmospheric pressure. But oxygen molecules are not easily soluble in liquids or water, which is what most of your blood is. Only 1.5 per cent of all the oxygen in your blood is actually dissolved. The rest has to be literally carried through the blood to the tissues. That job is done by the molecule haemoglobin, which is present in red blood cells.

Haemoglobin

Haemoglobin is made of three parts—two protein parts called alpha-globins and beta-globins, and an organic molecule called haeme. At the centre of each haeme molecule is an iron atom. The chemistry of haemoglobin makes the iron in the haeme very attractive to oxygen. As blood enters deep inside the lungs, the haemoglobin molecules take up oxygen very quickly to become **oxyhaemoglobin**.

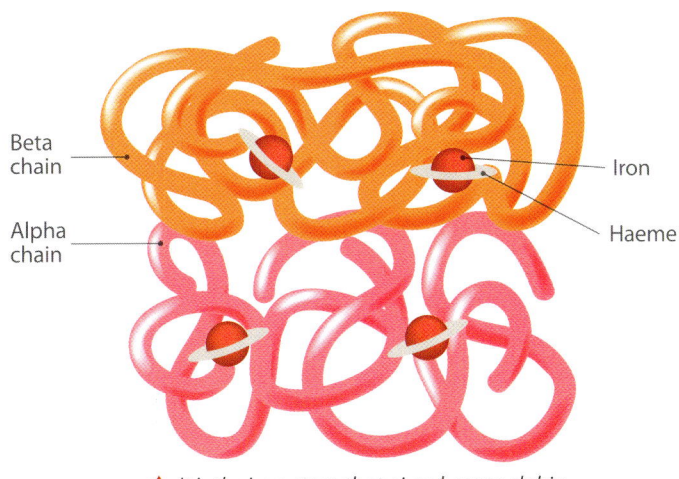
▲ *It is the iron atom that gives haemoglobin (and therefore blood) its bright red colour*

Delivering Oxygen

When oxygenated blood reaches the tissues, it reaches a place low in oxygen and high in acidity. The chemistry of haemoglobin now changes and oxygen is released. It diffuses from the plasma, into the cells, where it is taken up for respiration.

Haemoglobin and oxygen break up faster under higher temperatures. During exercise, muscle tissues release a lot of energy and heat up. Haemoglobin going to the muscles thus gives up oxygen more easily.

Carbon Monoxide

Haemoglobin is attracted even more to carbon monoxide (CO) than to oxygen. CO is a colourless odourless gas that is often found in the exhausts of vehicles and central heating furnaces. It forms carboxyhaemoglobin in the blood, which does not break up in the tissues. When a person inhales CO, they get headaches, feel dizzy and have pain in the chest. They can die quickly as their tissues (especially in the brain) die of oxygen starvation. If you suspect a person of having CO poisoning, switch off all flames and electrical devices. Take the person outdoors.

Incredible Individuals

John Scott Haldane (1860–1936) was a scientist concerned with the safety of coalmine workers, many of whom died of poisoning deep in the mines. He discovered that this was because of carbon monoxide. He published a report on safety in mines which got translated into many languages. He also designed a respirator that would prevent gas poisoning and studied the effect of very high altitude on breathing. (*see pp 18*)

▲ *Carbon monoxide is called the silent killer because it can neither be seen nor smelled*

Oxygen and Carbon Dioxide Cycles

At sea level, the atmosphere has a pressure of 760 mm Hg. All of us are adapted to breathe in this pressure (*see pp 17*). But the atmosphere is made of many gases, each of which has its own pressure, called its partial pressure.

Partial Pressure

Air in the alveolus is a mix of fresh air coming in and carbon dioxide being given out by blood. Therefore, the partial pressures of atmospheric gases are different from those in the open air. Under Boyle's Law, if two chambers filled with a gas are connected (here, the atmosphere and your lungs), the gas will move from one chamber to the other to make its partial pressures equal. Even if you did not actively breathe, oxygen would enter the lungs and carbon dioxide would leave. This is how the gills of fish and tracheae of insects work.

Gas	Outside the Body		Inside the Lungs	
	Percent of Air	Partial Pressure in mm Hg	Percent of Air	Partial Pressure in mm Hg
Nitrogen (N_2)	78.6	597.4	74.9	569
Oxygen (O_2)	20.9	158.8	13.7	104
Water vapour (H_2O)	0.04	3.0	6.2	40
Carbon dioxide (CO_2)	0.004	0.3	5.2	47
Others	0.0006	0.5	–	–
Total	100	760.0	100	760.0

Henry's Law

Henry's Law is a law of physics that states that the amount of gas in a liquid depends on its solubility in the liquid, and its partial pressure. Nitrogen has higher partial pressure than oxygen in alveolar air, but it is less soluble in water than oxygen. That is why it does not enter the blood. The partial pressure of O_2 in the alveolus (104 mm Hg) is higher than that in the capillaries bringing deoxygenated blood (40 mm Hg). Oxygen rushes into the capillaries, where it is taken up by haemoglobin. As the capillaries exit, the partial pressure rises up to 100 mm Hg.

In the tissues, the pressures change. For example, the partial pressure of oxygen in muscle tissue is only 20 mm Hg. Oxygen breaks up from haemoglobin and enters the muscle. Fat tissues use up a lot of oxygen, so it has high partial pressure of oxygen; and very little oxygen is released there.

Bohr Effect

The scientist Christian Bohr noticed that high acidity makes haemoglobin give up oxygen easily. As tissues make energy from glucose, they release CO_2. This enters the blood plasma, where it becomes carbonic acid:

$$H_2O + CO_2 \rightarrow H_2CO_3 \rightarrow H^+ + HCO_3^-$$

By the **Bohr effect**, the tissues get oxygen in exchange for carbon dioxide. Other acids, like lactic acid, which is produced during **anaerobic respiration** in the muscles, also make it happen.

 # Carbon Dioxide

Around 70 per cent of the carbon dioxide travels from tissues to lungs as bicarbonate ion. The enzyme carbonic anhydrase in the lungs breaks bicarbonate into water and carbon dioxide, which diffuses out.

$$H^+ + HCO_3^- \rightarrow H_2O + CO_2$$

About 20 per cent binds to haemoglobin as **carbamino-haemoglobin**, while the remaining 10 per cent dissolves in the plasma.

> ### Isn't It Amazing!
> While at rest, we consume approximately 250 millilitres (about 15 cubic inches) of oxygen each minute.

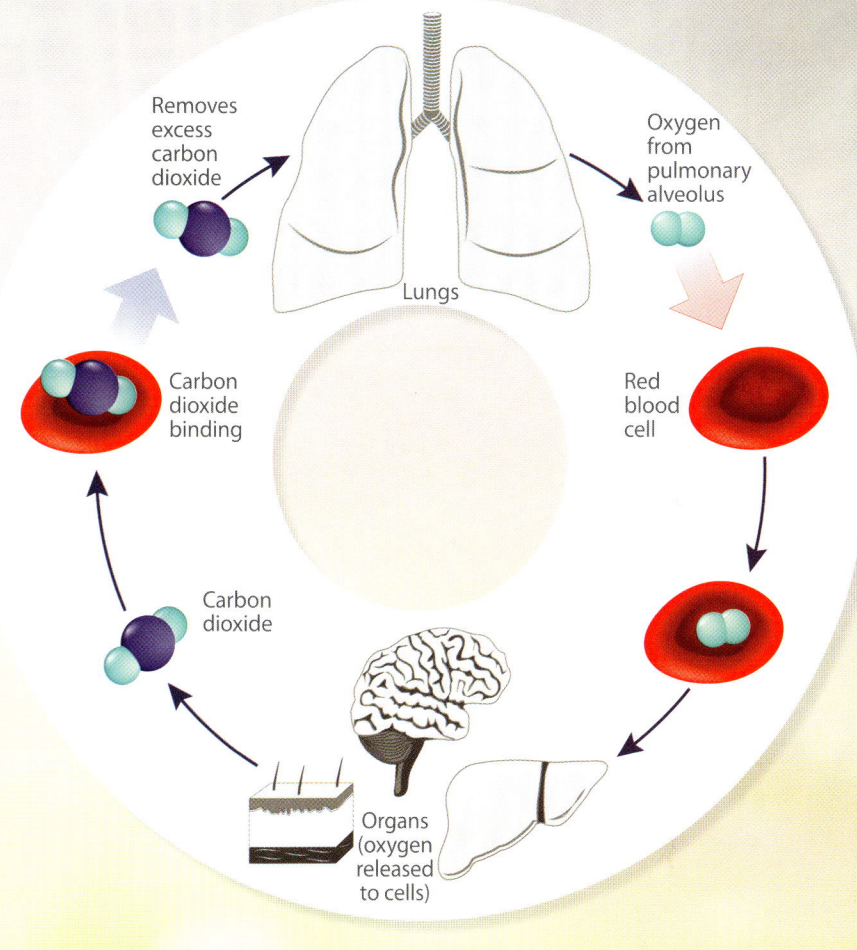

▲ The diagram shows the respiration process in human beings and the path of the red blood cells

Cellular Respiration

The word respiration has two meanings. When doctors and scientists talk about the whole body, they mean breathing in air (inspiration) or breathing it out (expiration). But when they talk about each cell of your body, respiration has a different meaning. It means how your cells convert their main fuel (glucose) into energy. When glucose is chemically broken down by the enzymes in your cells, it releases heat. This heat is used to make another chemical called Adenosine Triphosphate (ATP). Whenever the body needs quick energy, like when you exercise, the ATP is broken up and the heat stored is released again.

▲ *You need to watch your breathing while exercising*

Glycolysis

The first step of respiration is glycolysis, in which glucose is broken in a series of reactions into a smaller compound called pyruvate. If the cell has time, it will then carry out aerobic respiration. If the cell is in a hurry, as muscles cells are when you are running, it will carry out anaerobic respiration.

Aerobic Respiration

The oxygen you breathe in is used for aerobic respiration, in which glucose is broken down completely into carbon dioxide and water. Pyruvate goes through the Citric Acid Cycle (also called Krebs Cycle), a series of chemical reactions that turn it into NADH and $FADH_2$. These react with oxygen to form ATP and release CO_2.

Anaerobic Respiration

When the cell needs energy fast, it only carries out glycolysis and the pyruvate is turned into lactic acid instead. Less ATP is made, so you run out of energy fast (tiredness). The lactic acid is sent to the liver, where it is turned back into glucose, while you are resting.

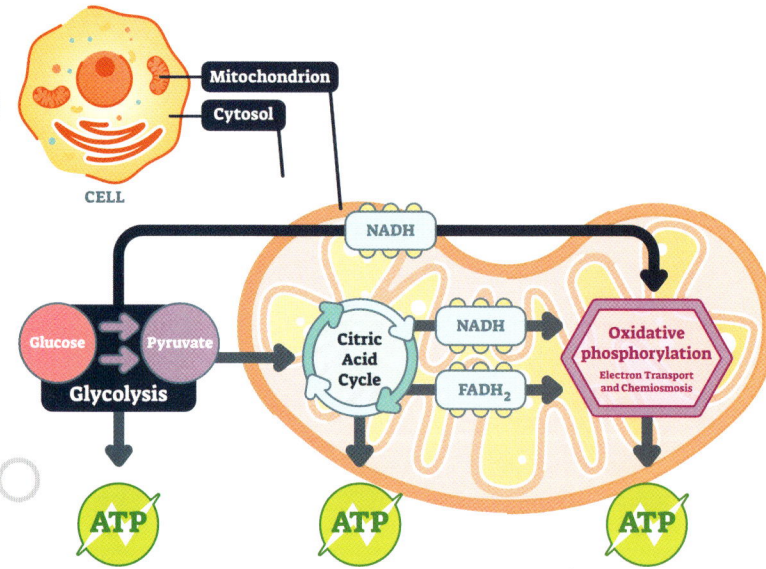

▲ *The diagram shows the process of aerobic respiration*

▼ *Cheeses made around the world are made by the process of fermentation*

💡 Isn't It Amazing!

Some bacteria can respire only anaerobically. They are useful to us in making cheese and yoghurt from milk. The lactic acid that is produced makes milk congeal. This is called fermentation.

| HUMAN BODY | LUNGS & RESPIRATORY SYSTEM | 17 |

Breathing Underwater

Human beings cannot breathe underwater as water would flood our lungs and drown us. So, what do the creatures that live underwater do? If life is impossible without oxygen, how do they procure it?

 ## Surviving Underwater

If divers go too deep without compressed air, they can get a condition called diver's bends. It is a condition which begins when they go deeper underwater and the pressure on their lungs increases. The nitrogen from their lungs dissolves in their blood and gets into fatty tissues. If they come up too quickly, the nitrogen comes out of the solution, forming bubbles in the body. These bubbles cause joint pains, paralysis and lack of muscle coordination (diver's staggers). Doctor's call this decompression sickness. If you go deep water diving, surface slowly by rising about a foot, staying for some time, and rising again, till you are in the safe zone.

▶ *The diagram shows how gills work. Fish also have lungs, but these have evolved into swim bladders that help them float*

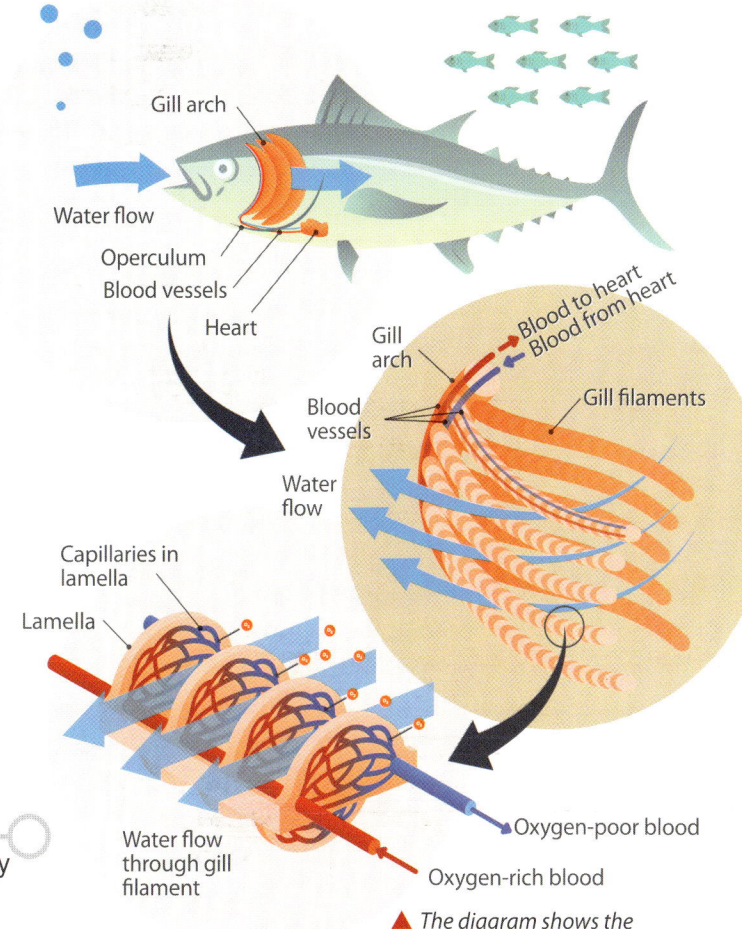

▲ *The diagram shows the respiratory system of a fish*

 ## Breathing Apparatuses

Animals like sponges and jellyfish filter the oxygen directly from the water, often filling it in a body cavity called **coelom**. Most fishes have gills, which are organs that filter oxygen from water. The development of a circulatory system with haemoglobin helped speed up the body's intake of oxygen in fish. They take in water from the mouth and pass it through gill arches. Each arch is made of fine gill filaments, which have blood capillaries that filter oxygen. The gills are covered by a flap of skin called **operculum**. Lungs begin to develop in amphibians when they change from tadpoles to adults. From here onwards, the animal filters oxygen from air rather than water.

In Real Life

Octopus gills can extract as much as 80 per cent of the oxygen from seawater.

▶ *Octopus*

Incredible Individuals

Early divers' equipment required them to be attached to a long tube from which air was pumped from a ship overhead. Jacques Cousteau invented the portable aqualung in 1943, which made it possible for divers to swim freely underwater. He also made many award-winning movies and TV shows that made underwater diving a popular sport.

▲ *A diver is getting ready to jump into the water*

Breathing at High Altitudes

As we go higher up and above sea level, the amount of oxygen in the air drops. Because of this, the partial pressure of oxygen entering our lungs also falls. At altitudes over 2400 m, like in the Himalayas or the Andes mountains, oxygen is 60 per cent less than at sea level. Mountaineers and trekkers experience what they call altitude sickness, if they climb the mountain too quickly.

◀ Himalayan mountaineers carry pressurised oxygen cylinders to minimise altitude sickness

Altitude Sickness

Enough oxygen does not enter the blood from the lungs, and so the tissues experience oxygen starvation. Patients experience shortness of breath and panting, headaches, sleeplessness and reduced vision and hearing. They may get chest pains or vomiting. They must be brought to a lower place immediately. Slowly ascending the mountains helps keep away altitude sickness by letting the body '**acclimatise**'.

Andeans

The people of the Andean plateau in Bolivia also live at very high altitudes. But they have adapted differently. They have more RBCs in their blood, so they can get more oxygen out of the lungs than people at sea level can. They also have more haemoglobin, so they can pull in more oxygen from the lungs. The people of the Ethiopian Plateau in Africa have similar adaptations.

Tibetans

The people of Tibet have lived at altitudes of over 4000 m for generations. So how do they not get altitude sickness? They have larger lungs than others and can inhale and exhale more air in a breath than most of us can. This does not tire them out. The lungs thus store more air, and more oxygen goes into their blood.

▼ Tibetans have lived at high altitudes for over 25,000 years

▲ Through different means, Andeans and Tibetans get enough oxygen in their blood

★ Incredible Individuals

In 1999, Babu Chhiri Sherpa lived on the world's highest point for 21 hours. That is right! He was on Mount Everest without canned oxygen. Doctors call any point above 8000 m the death zone.

Asthma

Anyone can get asthma, especially children. When an 'asthmatic attack' happens, the patient gets **bronchospasms**. This is a sudden constriction of the tubes that reduces the volume of air entering the lungs. Allergens like dust, pollen or spores, pet hair, dander and tobacco smoke, as well as weather changes and heavy exercise, can set off an asthma attack.

Symptoms of Asthma

The main symptoms of asthma are shortness of breath and wheezing, sometimes coughing. If the face turns a bluish colour, the pulse quickens and the patient seems confused or anxious, rush them to a doctor. Asthma cannot be cured completely. It can often be managed by avoiding the allergen and using a drug nebuliser.

How Asthma Happens

Asthma is usually an allergic reaction to something that the patient encounters repeatedly. This causes bronchospasms, where the walls and mucosa of the air tubes become inflamed and swollen. Cells of the immune system, such as eosinophils and neutrophils, rush into the lamina propria in high numbers. There is also swelling of the mucus in the bronchi or bronchioles, triggering wheezing.

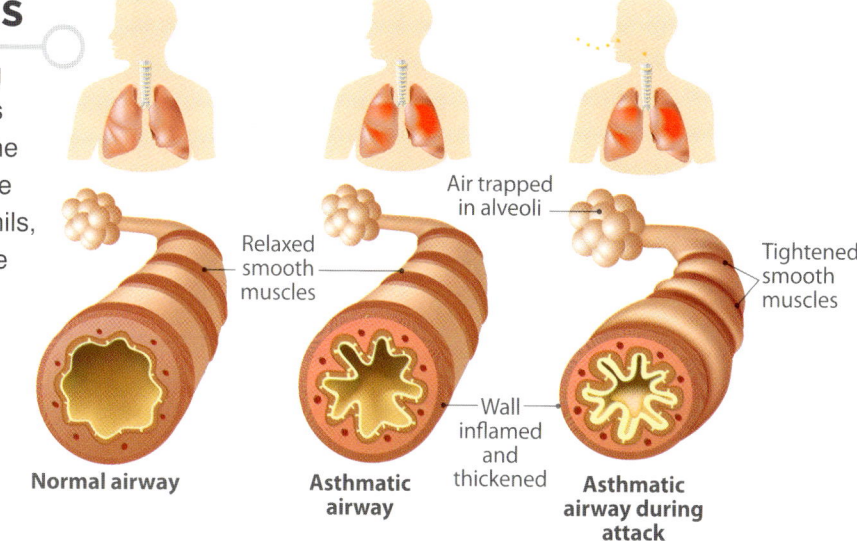

▲ The main symptom of asthma is wheezing, a forced whistling sound from the airpipe

In Real Life

Inhalation as a therapy is as old as 1554 BCE! The ancient Egyptian 'Ebers papyrus', now in the University of Leipzig, records that doctors would heat bricks and then throw cuttings of the herb black henbane on them. The patient would be made to inhale the emitted vapours, which restored their breath.

Wheezing

Wheezing is the first sign of breathing problems like choking, COPD or asthma, along with the heaving of the chest. It is also common among smokers and may be triggered by an allergic shock.

If you get wheezing, take your medicines and get to a warm, moist area or breathe in steam from an inhaler. Get to an emergency room if the wheezing goes on for some time, and your skin feels blue (which is a sign that there is not enough oxygen in the blood). You may need blood tests, asthma checks and lung function tests.
(see pp 22)

▶ Asthma is one of the most frequent causes of hospitalisation among children

▲ Henbane is a toxic herb; modern doctors do not recommend it to anyone

Poison in the Air

Anything in the air that should not naturally be there is a pollutant. Outdoor pollution is the result of burning gasoline and coal. It is also caused by releasing gases like sulphur dioxide, nitrogen oxides, carbon monoxide, ozone and smoke in high quantities. Indoor pollution happens because of carbon monoxide from central heating, chemical sprays, asbestos, insect droppings, spores, pollen, and most importantly, tobacco smoke. These can cause asthma, chronic obstructive pulmonary disease, heart and blood diseases and cancers leading to death. Pregnant women are at danger of pre-term birth and giving birth to babies with **congenital diseases**. Climate change is causing an increase in air pollution, with rising dust, mould and ozone levels.

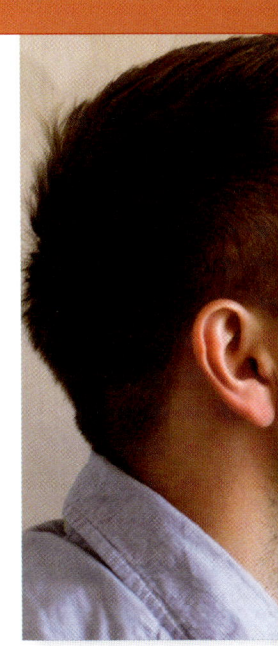

Lung Cancer

Though many people take up smoking, medical research has shown that there is no benefit from it. 3 out of every 10 people who get cancer, get it because of tobacco. The Centers for Disease Control and Prevention says that smoking causes 87 per cent of all deaths because of lung or colorectal cancer. It leaves patients at high risk of heart disease and stroke. Inhaling another person's smoke is no better. 7300 adults die, each year, of lung cancer because a friend or family member was a heavy smoker.

Lung cancer happens when lung cells go out of the body's control. It develops in four stages and cannot be cured if detected too late. In the fourth stage, it becomes **metastatic**. Here, the cancer cells spread to other organs and damage them, especially the lymph nodes. Small cell lung cancers have cancerous cells that look smaller than others under a microscope. People with this kind of cancer have to be treated with radiation therapy and chemotherapy. Non-small cell lung cancers are more common, the cells look bigger under the microscope. Doctors can remove them surgically if found early enough.

A person with lung cancer is generally short of breath, wheezes and coughs all the time, and often coughs up blood. They feel tired all the time and experience pain in the chest. They lose weight very fast.

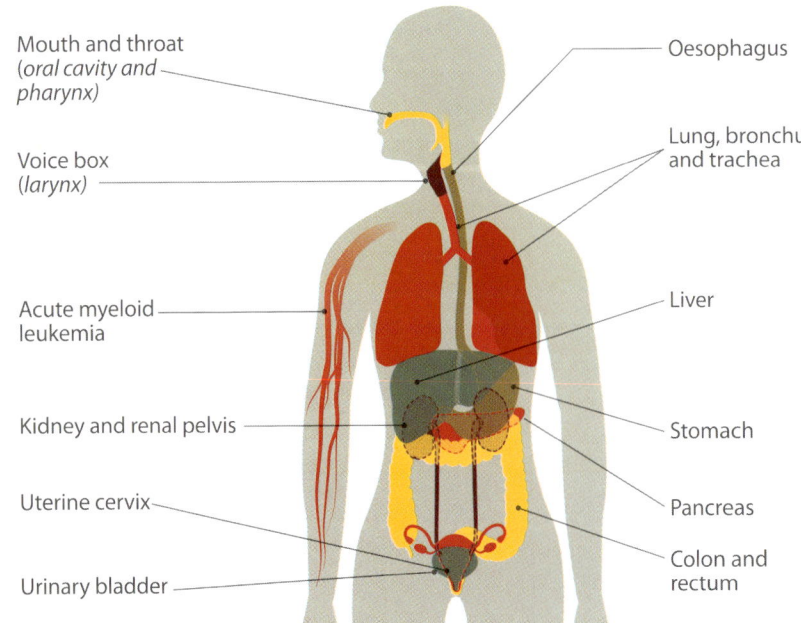

Tobacco use causes cancer throughout the body

▲ *If you know someone who smokes, tell them to stop now*

In Real Life

The year 1952 was toxic for the people of London. From December 5 to 9, upto 12,000 people died because of fog mixed with smoke from coal fires that descended on the London air.

Chronic Obstructive Pulmonary Disease (COPD)

This is a disease that makes it hard for patients to breathe. It was earlier called bronchitis, but now doctors also include damage to the lung (**emphysema**) as a condition. Most people with COPD get it from smoking too much. Very few people may also get it genetically.

Air pollution, factory fumes and cooking on log fires also cause COPD. Patients experience dry cough (no mucus), tiredness, repeated infections of the lungs or nose, and shortness of breath after even mild work. They may develop cardiac problems if untreated for too long. Doctors use a machine called a spirometer to check for COPD.

COPD cannot be cured. Quitting smoking stops it from becoming worse, and the patient may use an inhaler whenever they get short of breath. Some patients may need to breathe from an oxygen tank. Walking and breathing exercises also help *(see pp 30)*.

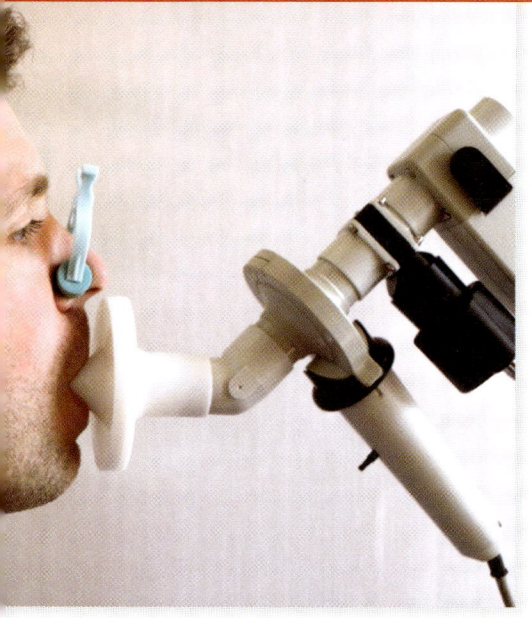

▲ *Spirometers measure how hard it is to breathe. Doctors call it a Pulmonary Function Test*

Respirators and Gas Masks

With a rise in pollution in many cities around the world, doctors recommend using breathing masks. These masks filter out pollutants and dust from the air before they can reach your mouth and nose. N95 respirators are recommended by the US Centers for Disease Control and Prevention for people in dangerous workplaces such as mines, construction sites and chemical plants.

On the other hand, most gas masks are designed to keep away specific poisonous gases before they can reach you. Many of these masks contain activated carbon, which absorbs certain harmful substances. Gas masks are used by soldiers, firemen and other emergency workers to go into dangerous areas. High Efficiency Particulate Air (HEPA) masks are suggested for people who may have allergies from pollen and other airborne substances, and for doctors and nurses dealing with airborne viral diseases such as Ebola. Before you put on a gas mask, you must ask your doctor to recommend the one that is right for you.

▲ *Smog causes poor visibility, burning in the eyes and wheezing*

◄ *Passive smoking is really harmful for children*

Under the Weather

We have all got it, perhaps many times in life. Sneezing, a sore throat, a stuffy or runny nose and coughing—there is nothing uncommon about a cold. While some people believe that a cold will go away on its own, a cold left untreated can become an attack of **influenza**. This can be very serious, requiring you to be admitted to a hospital. Let us understand how, and why you get the common cold.

What is a Cold?

Cold is actually your immune system's common response to different types of viral infections. You catch them by breathing in infected air, touching unclean surfaces that have been touched by an infected person, or by being in contact with a person with a cold.

When you have a cold, your respiratory system makes a lot of mucus to trap the germs in. When you cough, it comes out as **phlegm**, a thickened form of the mucus. Make sure that you wash away the phlegm or incinerate the tissues you have coughed into. You may also get a lot of tears as they remove germs from your eyes. You get a sore throat because the lamina propria swells up with immune cells, and lymph as they fight the germs.

Dealing with Cold

Regularly wash your hands and keep your home, school or office clean to keep all types of cold away. If you have a cold, stay at home, get lots of rest and do not meet people. Drink a lot of soup and juices (but not coffee or colas). Gargle out the soreness in your throat with warm, salted water. Antivirals, medicines that kill viruses, may help you control the infection. Cold often makes way for bacterial infections like bronchitis or sinusitis, so you may need antibiotics too. Other medicines, which your doctor might suggest, are:

- Expectorants, which loosen the mucus and make it easier to breathe.
- Cough suppressants that stop you from coughing.
- Nasal decongestants, that unblock the nose.
- Antihistamines, which reduce swelling of the throat and stop sneezing.
- Pain relievers, which soothe headaches and throat pain.

▶ *A thermometer is used to measure your body's temperature and to check if you are ill*

Influenza

A cold can easily lead to influenza or flu. Patients of influenza get fevers, chills, body aches and feel tired. They feel grumpy all the time and may feel like vomiting. Often they also have a runny nose. Most people can get over flu without medicine, but children under the age of 5 or people over 65, pregnant women and people with asthma, diabetes or lung diseases need treatment.

▶ *Small children with colds should not be given aspirin or cough medicine*

Viruses and Vaccines

There are four types of influenza viruses, namely A, B, C and D. Influenza viruses also exist as hundreds of strains. Influenza A is the most infectious and has caused many **pandemics** or outbreaks of disease all over the world. The Spanish flu of 1918 killed nearly 100 million people! Luckily, there are vaccines against them now, and you should get them every year.

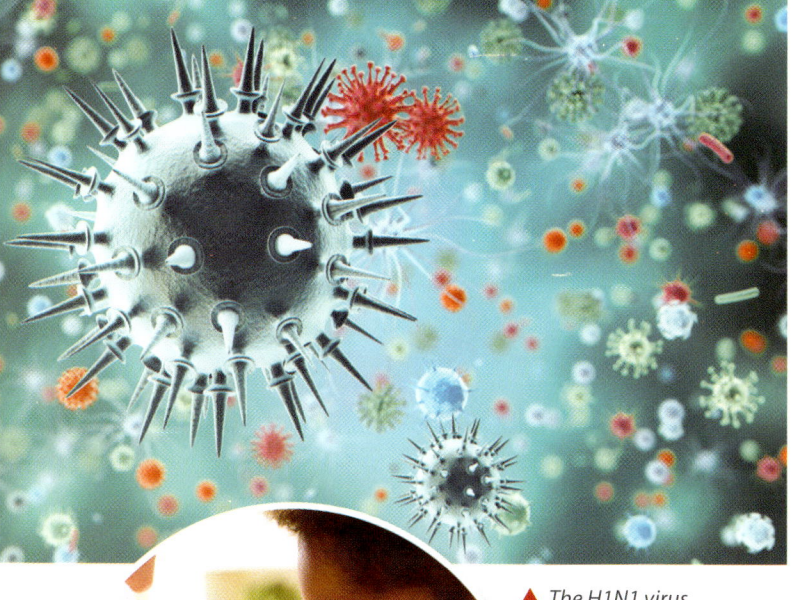

▲ The H1N1 virus. A new strain called swine flu became a pandemic in 2009

Incredible Individuals

During the 2009 swine flu pandemic, the World Health Organisation had predicted that 2 billion people would get infected worldwide. Former US President Barack Obama got himself vaccinated to encourage people to get the vaccine. It was also a way to discourage a growing 'anti-vaccine' movement, where people believed that vaccinating themselves or their children would lead to autism.

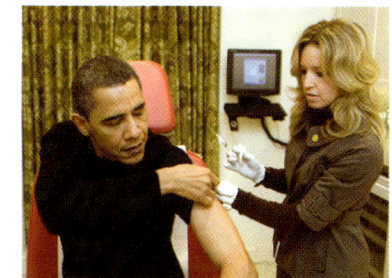

◀ Former US President Barrack Obama getting a vaccine injection

 ## Measles

Fever, red and watery eyes, a dripping nose and severe congestion of the throat and nose—these are the signs that somebody might have measles. It is easily confused with common cold and most people know it only when a rash develops on the skin, and bluish-white spots appear on the tongue. There is no effective cure for it, but babies who have been vaccinated will never get it. In the USA, Europe and Australia, the disease has mostly been eliminated, though it exists in Africa and Asia.

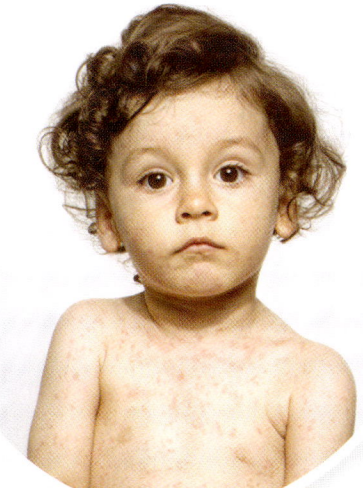

▶ A baby boy infected with measles

◀ Flu masks are important for preventing the spread of infection

In Real Life

Psittacosis is a disease that you can get by inhaling germs from the dried-up droppings of pigeons and other birds. It can cause a cough, headache and vomiting.

 ## Reye Syndrome

Reye Syndrome is a condition in some children who have suffered from influenza or chicken pox. There is a higher risk if the child was treated with aspirin. It causes swelling in the brain, vomiting, and a feeling of tiredness all the time. Children with this syndrome feel confused and dizzy and may be left with permanent brain damage. In very serious cases, they may get seizures, inability to breathe and may go into a coma. Sadly, we know of no treatment for it.

Invaders of Your Lungs

The respiratory system has many defences against germs— the mucus in the lining of the inner nose, the pharynx, trachea and bronchial tree, trap germs. The cilia brush them out of the respiratory system. Special tissues called NALT and BALT, and immune cells in the bronchi act as spies against germs. They bring in more immune cells to destroy them. Yet, some bacteria and viruses can make it past, like the influenza virus. Let us see what some of them do, and how the body fights back.

▲ Immune cells called macrophages in the alveoli destroy any germs that still make it to the lungs

▼ You shouldn't ignore your coughs. If you keep coughing for 2 days or more, visit the doctor

Tuberculosis (TB)

Historically called consumption, this disease is caused due to an infection of the lungs by *mycobacterium tuberculosis*. Once a major scourge of the world, it is on the wane, though still deadly. You can get it if you have a weak immune system, and come in contact with someone who has the disease already, and they cough, sneeze or talk to you without covering their face.

You may have TB if you have been:
- coughing for three weeks or more,
- coughing up blood,
- having fever and sweating at night,
- losing weight and not feeling hungry,
- feeling weak and tired.

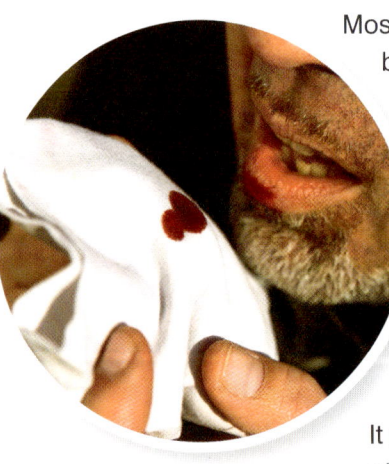

▲ Coughing up blood is a symptom of tuberculosis

Most people who get the bacterium will not get the disease. But they may not be able to get rid of it either. This is called latent TB. If their immune system becomes weak, such as after an organ transplant, a major illness or HIV infection, then the TB bacterium starts growing. It makes holes in the lungs and other organs, called lesions.

Isn't It Amazing!

Cattle can also contract tuberculosis. Some scientists are of the view that human beings got tuberculosis from cows, especially in the Neolithic Period when they domesticated cattle. However, some other scientists disagree with this observation. Others, however, think that they may have got it separately.

The Poets' Disease

In the 19th century, without a cure available, people died a slow death from TB. Poets and writers wrote of their impending death and suffering, from John Keats and P.B. Shelley (who died of it), to Leo Tolstoy and Anton Chekhov, whose characters usually had it. After Robert Koch discovered the bacterial cause of TB, and the BCG vaccine was developed later, literature became more hopeful again. TB is now curable through a combination of drugs that you need to take for six months to a year.

▲ John Keats

▲ P. B. Shelley

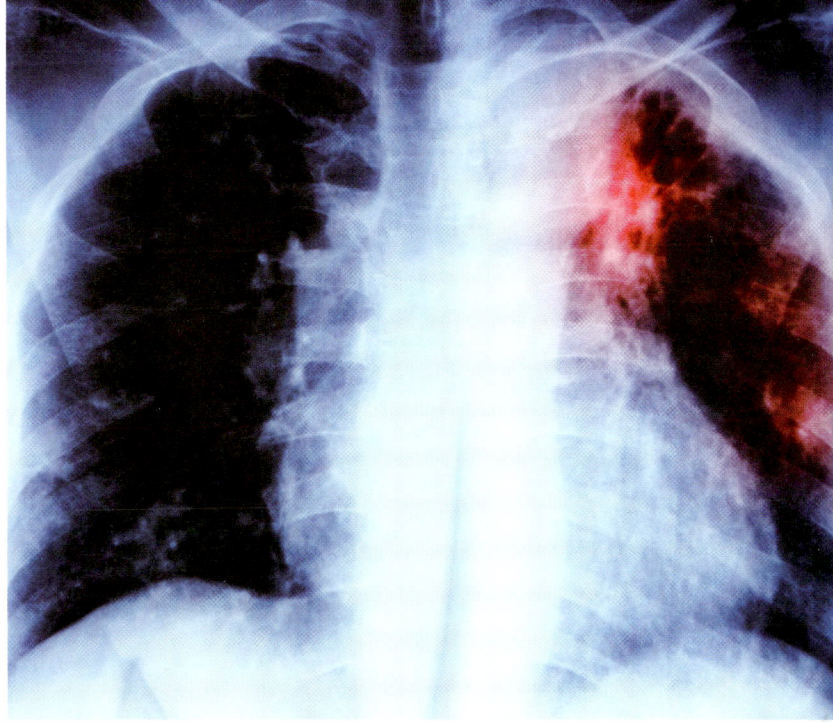

▲ An x-ray of the chest, showing TB lesions in the lungs (coloured in)

Pneumonia

Pneumonia is caused by many bacteria invading your lungs, especially *Streptococcus pneumoniae* (pneumococcus). It is very serious in smokers, old people and children under the age of five, though others get it too. Pneumonia feels like a cold at the start: with coughs, fever and wheezing. If the fever continues, with chills, chest pain and cough with phlegm, you may have gotten pneumonia.
The disease gets severe if the bacteria enter the blood, from where they can get to the brain, causing meningitis.

What keeps colds away *(see pp 16–17)* also keeps pneumonia away. Doctors treat pneumonia with antibiotics and rest.

▶ Wearing facemasks can help you avoid breathing in germs

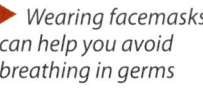

Incredible Individuals

President William Henry Harrison of the USA caught a cold on 26 March 1841. Unable to rest, his cold turned to pneumonia, and he died nine days later. He had only become president on 4 March.

▶ William Henry Harrison

Pertussis

Pertussis is also called whooping cough. It is a major cause of child deaths in some countries of Africa and Asia, though it has been nearly eliminated in the USA and Europe. It is caused by the bacterium *Bordetella pertussis*. Its symptoms are similar to that of a cold: a dry cough and fever. Then they get 'whoops', when they cough terribly followed by a whistling sound when they breathe. In small children, it may lead to periods when they cannot breathe at all. However, babies who are given the DPT vaccines never get it.

Exercises to Breathe Better

Stress, poor sleep and lack of exercise affect the way you breathe. This is also true for diseases like COPD. Over time, stale air collects in your lungs and leaves you gasping for breath. By doing breathing exercises, you can clear out your lungs, while inhaling fresh air. This eases your muscles and brings more oxygen to your tissues.

Breathing exercises do not replace medical treatments, but can help ease discomfort and help healthy people avoid illnesses. They also help you take time off work or study, and help relax your muscles. This practice of relaxation is called meditation. It is widely practised in Asian countries. Good ventilation, regular sleep and a balanced diet also help your respiratory health.

▲ *Taking a few minutes off, every hour, to do breathing exercises helps you beat stress*

Pursed Lip Breathing

Get to a calm, quiet place. Sit down comfortably and relax your arms and legs. Inhale through your nose. Exhale through your mouth, with the lips held close, for twice as long.

 Pranayama

This is an ancient breathing exercise from India. Here is the simplest way to do it—put your finger on one nostril and breathe in deeply and slowly till your chest has expanded fully. Hold onto the air you have breathed for a minute, then exhale it slowly till your chest is compressed fully. Breathe in again. Pranayama helps remove CO_2 effectively, but you must do it only when guided by an instructor till you are trained enough.

◀ *Pranayama is part of an Indian system of mind and body training called yoga*

Belly Breathing

Lie down comfortably on your back and loosen your muscles. Keep your hands on your belly and press them down gently. Breathe in deeply and slowly, through your nose. Breathe out through the mouth for twice as long.

▼ *Belly breathing helps exercise your diaphragm*

In Real Life

Some people begin to breathe very fast when they are worried or excited. This is called **hyperventilation**. The effect of hyperventilation can be reduced in a person by practising the following exercise with them: ask them to breathe while you say slowly '1, 2, breathe in', and '3, 4, breathe out'.

Your Body's Sound Box

Just below the epiglottis, where the trachea begins, is your larynx. It is also known as the voice box. Made of cartilage and muscles, it has an interesting structure that allows you to make sounds. Human beings have among the most complex larynges, which allow them to make dozens of different sounds. They can string the sounds together to make words and sentences. Also, this includes all the grunts and hisses you make when you are too busy to reply properly to someone. But did you know that your larynx develops from the same tissue that, in fish, becomes gills? Such organs are called evolutionary homologues.

Structure

If you feel your throat, you will realise it is hard, though not as hard as a bone. This is where the voice box is, made of three pieces of cartilage—the epiglottis (see pp 6–7), thyroid cartilage and cricoid cartilage. The thyroid cartilage is bigger in men and can be felt easily. It is called Adam's apple. The cricoid cartilage is thicker and ring-shaped. Three small pairs of cartilage are attached to the epiglottis—the arytenoids, corniculates and cuneiforms—that help move the vocal cords.

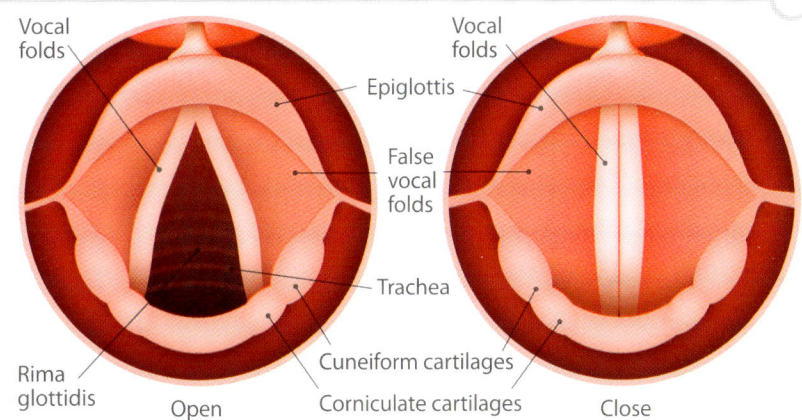

Below the epiglottis is the glottis, made of folds of tissue called the true vocal cords and the false vocal cords. True vocal cords are thin and membranous, held in place by the cartilages and vocal muscles. As air passes, they vibrate like guitar strings to make sound. Men have broader cords that give them a deeper voice, while women have narrower ones, so they sound different from men.

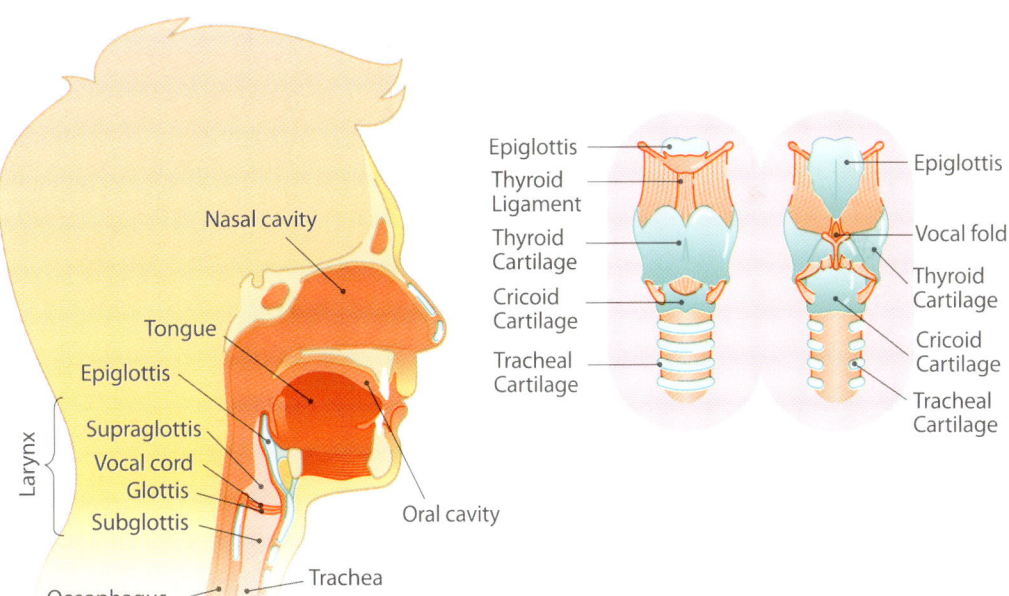

▲ The vocal folds close when we speak, so that the air going out makes them vibrate

In Real Life

As teenage boys grow older, their larynx cartilages become ossified. Bone minerals deposited in them make them harder, making the voice box more resonant. Their nasal sinuses also grow bigger, giving more internal echo and that is also why your voice sounds deeper to you than it does to others.

▶ Adolescent male voice changes happen under the influence of the hormone testosterone

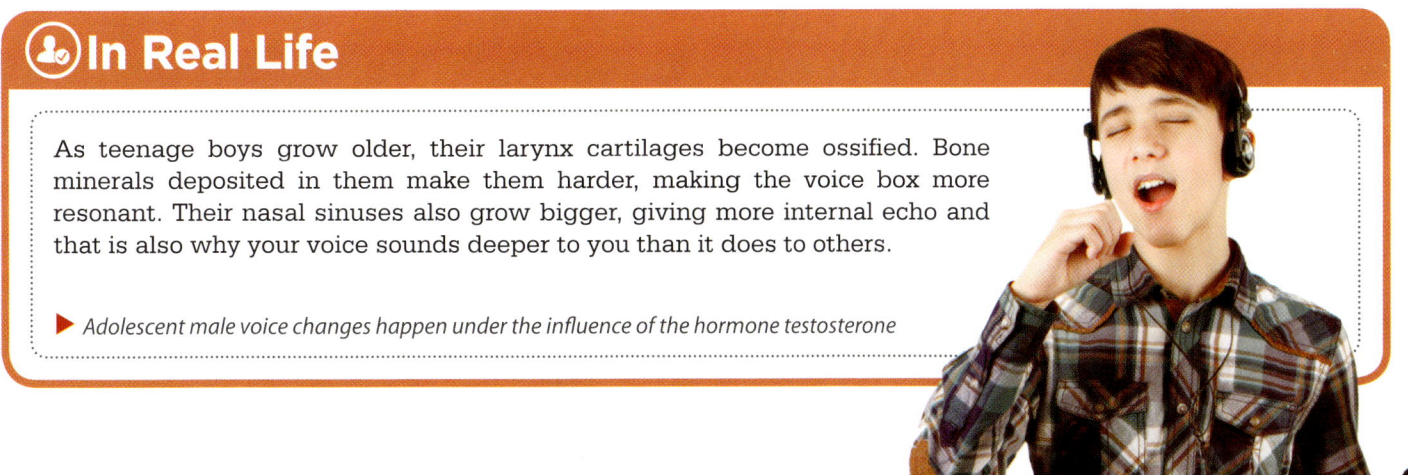

Making Words, Making Sense

Our larynx helps us make sounds, but how do we turn that into words and sentences? How does each language we speak have different sounds and different ways to combine those sounds into words and paragraphs?

Larynx

It turns out the larynx is not just complex, but very finely tuned, like a piano, to make dozens of sounds. It interacts with our tongue, pharynx, mouth, nasal cavity and even sinuses. This is how it makes sounds, pitches and tones. It can change them ever so slightly to make the same words tinged with different emotions. So, the same sentence can be a question, a statement, sarcasm or mockery.

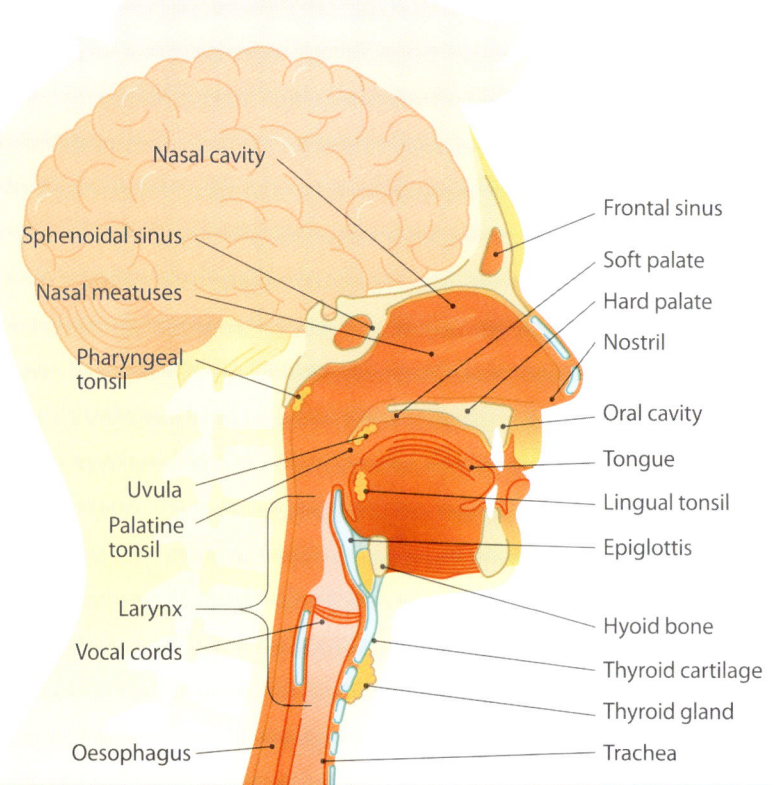

Different parts of the brain and respiratory system work together to make speech.

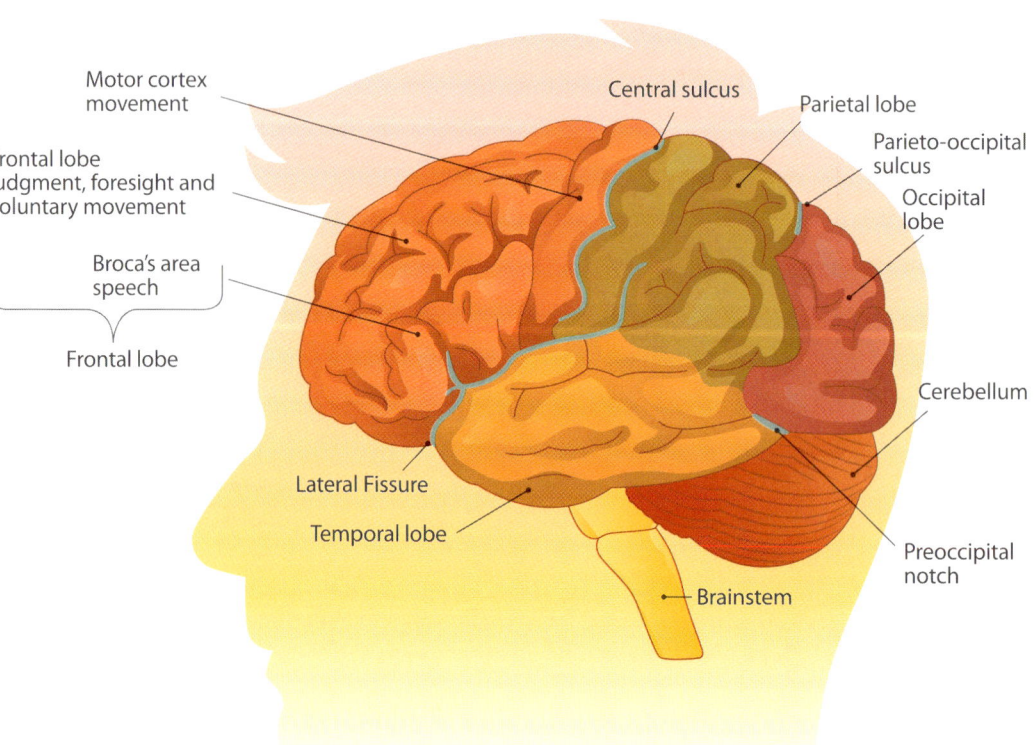

HUMAN BODY — LUNGS & RESPIRATORY SYSTEM

Laryngeal Muscles

The laryngeal muscles work with the brain to make sounds. The cricothyroid muscle pulls the cricoid and thyroid cartilages to the front, stretching and thinning the vocal cords. This raises the pitch of the sound as we talk. Other muscles contract the vocal cords to make deeper sounds, and a whole lot of other adjustments.

Vocal Folds

Your vocal folds are closed when breathing in and stretched out when breathing out. This lets you control your breathing when you are speaking.

Pharynx

As the vocal cords vibrate, the air passing through them vibrates with the same frequency. This air then resonates in the laryngopharynx above, before passing into the mouth. This helps you make unvoiced sounds, like 'cut', 'cheap', 'tub', 'thin' etc. It also helps make rough sounds like 'hat' and 'heat', or smooth ones like 'at' and 'eat', by restricting or easing the flow of air.

Organ	Name	Sound	Example
Lips	Labial	p, b	**p**at, **b**at
Tongue and Teeth	Dental	t, d	**t**ip, **d**ip
Tongue and palate (press hard)	Palatal	ch, j	**c**hoke, **j**oke
Tongue and palate (press gently)	Liquid	l, r	**l**oom, **r**oom
Back of throat	Velar	k, g	**c**rab, **g**rab

Tongue and Lips
Your tongue is very important in shaping the sounds that come out by the way it touches the pharynx, the roof of the mouth (palate) and the teeth. Labial sounds arise when the air is forced through the lips and comes out as a burst.

Diaphragm

It might be surprising, but your diaphragm also helps to make sounds. It turns your chest into a resonating cavity (like the box of a guitar). It creates sounds like 'gut', 'jeep', 'dub', 'this' or 'bun'.

Nose and Sinuses

The nose and its associated sinuses help you make the humming sounds 'm' and 'n'. To make the first, you keep the lips pressed and breathe out, you get a sound like 'mum'. Breathe out with your lips open and your tongue pressed to the teeth and you get 'nun'.

Cheeks and Jaws

Your cheeks and jaws shrink or expand your mouth cavity, and help you make vowels.

	Jaws shut	Jaws open
Cheeks shut	b**oo**t	b**oa**t
Cheeks open	b**ee**t	b**ai**t

Brain

The Broca's Area and Wernicke's Area in the cerebral cortex control speech and interact with the Hippocampus and frontal cortex to regulate memory, vocabulary, grammar and sentence formation. They send out motor signals through the midbrain and cerebellum to control how sounds are finally made.

Fluid in Your Lungs

Did you know that you could drown and die at the top of very high mountains? This is because of a condition called high altitude pulmonary oedema, in which the vessels in the lungs constrict, causing fluid to leak from the blood vessels to the tissues of the lungs. This condition occurs in lowlanders who ascend to higher altitude regions, usually above 2,500 to 3,000 feet, at a rapid pace. Let us find out what happens to a person when fluid enters their lungs, and how can their life be saved.

 ## Pulmonary Oedema

Doctors refer to any tissue becoming full of plasma or fluid as oedema. Pulmonary oedema (water in the lungs) happens because of too much blood pressure, too little alveolar pressure (like at high altitudes), or damage to the capillaries of the lungs due to injury or infection. Plasma from the blood fills the alveoli. The pulmonary surfactant is disturbed, and oxygen does not dissolve anymore. The patient will make a gurgling sound as they breathe and feel heavy in the chest. Without urgent medical help, the patient may die within 10 minutes.

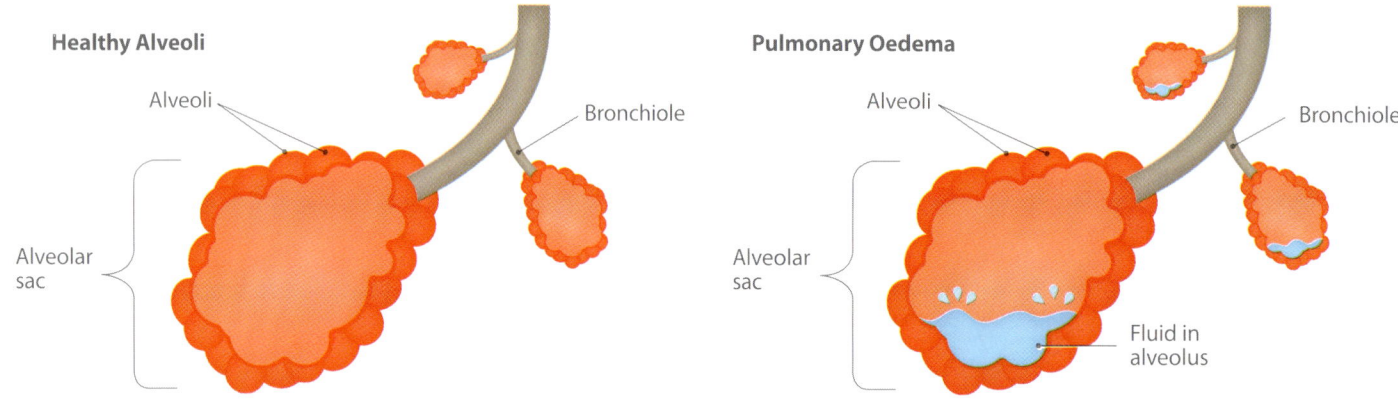

▲ Oedema is sometimes called internal drowning, but doctors do not use that term

 ## Congestion

Congestion happens when blood enters the lungs due to injury or infection. It may happen because of high blood pressure or failure of the left side of the heart.

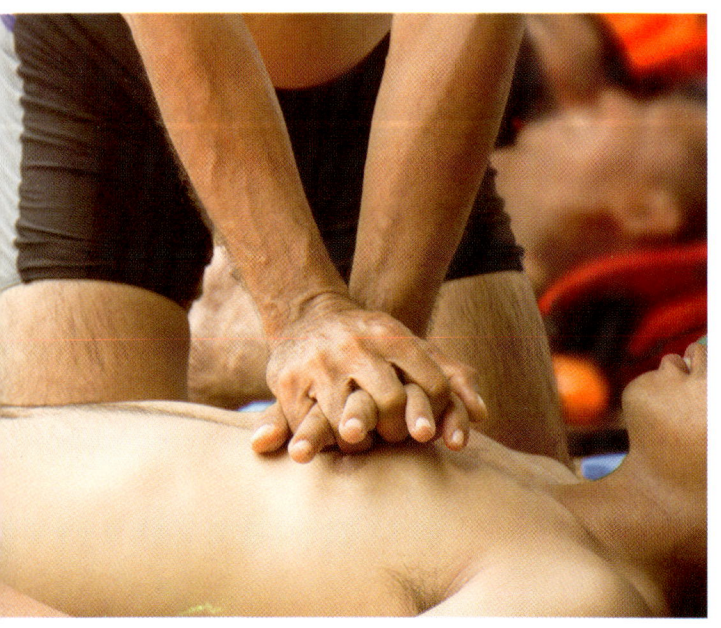

◀ Cardiopulmonary Resuscitation (CPR) is the first response for a drowning victim. Do not try to pump water from their lungs

Isn't It Amazing!

Diving into cold water triggers the mammalian diving reflex. Blood flows to the limbs and belly. More blood goes to the heart and brain. The heart rate also slows down.

 ## Drowning

Doctors define drowning as the process of experiencing respiratory impairment from submersion or immersion in liquid. Unlike oedema, water does not enter the lungs when a person is drowning, because the body triggers the **laryngospasm**. In this, the vocal cords shut off the airway, if they sense water coming in. Instead, the person dies from lack of air if they remain underwater for too long. If they become unconscious, the laryngospasm may relax, and water may enter their lungs, causing oedema.

HUMAN BODY | LUNGS & RESPIRATORY SYSTEM

Bringing Someone Back to Life

Many people can be brought back from near death by a few techniques, known as resuscitation. While all medical professionals are trained to do them, a few are simple enough that you too can learn to do them. Be ready to help anyone who may be in need. But you have to be careful and do it right, so it needs some practice. Remember that some may not be suitable for children, who may be hurt rather than helped. Always remember to call the emergency number immediately after you have done the procedures, so that the patient gets the right medical help.

Heimlich Manoeuvre

This was invented by Dr Henry Heimlich for helping people who have swallowed something and are choking. If the object is not removed from their throat, they can die. Do this only if the patient cannot help themselves. Grab them from behind and make a fist of one hand, thumb inward. Put it on their belly, put the other hand over it and squeeze hard. It pushes the diaphragm up, forcing air out of the lungs. Whatever was choking them gets spat out.

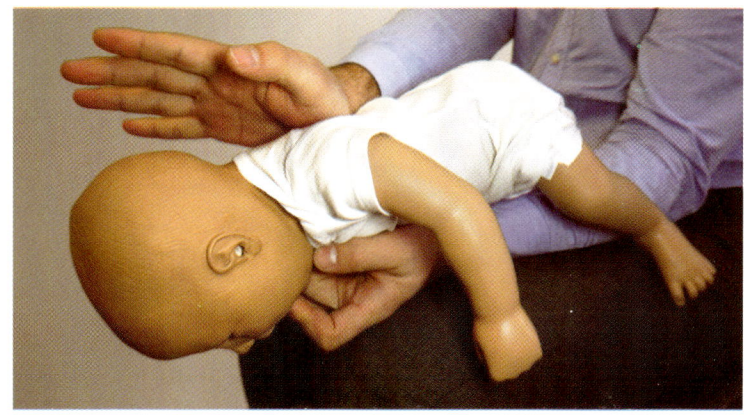
▲ Do not try the Heimlich manoeuvre on a healthy person. It can cause them cramps

Cardiopulmonary Resuscitation

Do this for someone who has fainted because of a heart attack. If their brain does not get oxygen soon, they can die. Lay them on the floor and press their chest down with both your palms, forcing them to gasp. Do this till they are able to breathe again, or until medical help arrives. If the victim still does not breathe, hold their mouth open, pinch their nose and blow air into it. This is mouth-to-mouth resuscitation, sometimes called the kiss of life.

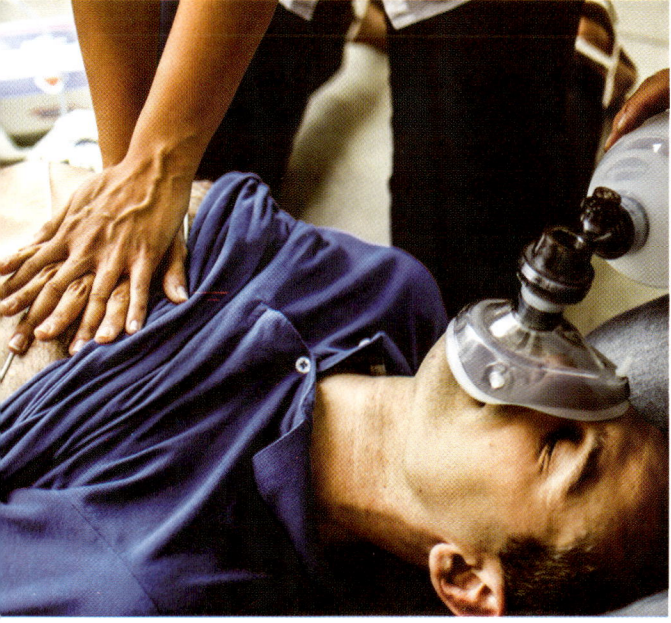
◀ Follow A-B-C during CPR: Open the airways, trigger breathing and let circulation happen

In Real Life

In extreme cases, doctors may recommend oxygen therapy for people with COPD or viral diseases. During this therapy, the patient is made to breathe pure oxygen, as opposed to air, which only has 21 per cent of the gas. Oxygen is stored in a pressurised cylinder and delivered through a special breathing tube. It does not reduce the damage to the lungs and other tissues caused by pollution, smoking or viral infections. But, it helps overcome shortage of breath and oxygen starvation in the tissues.

Incredible Individuals

When the famous artist Pablo Picasso was born, he was not breathing. The doctor, Don Salvador, had taken a smoke break. He rushed in and blew the smoke into Pablo's face, which brought him to life!

▶ Don Salvador

Word Check

Acclimatise: It is the practice of making the body get used to different weather conditions, especially high altitude.

Alveolar macrophage: It is an immune cell in the alveoli that destroys germs.

Alveolar pressure: It is the pressure of the mix of gases in the alveoli.

Alveoli: They are the functional units of the lungs where gas exchange happens.

Anaerobic respiration: They are the chemical reactions in cells that do not require oxygen to produce energy from glucose.

Bohr effect: It is the effect of acidity on the binding of oxygen to haemoglobin.

Boyle's Law: It is the law of physics that governs the relationship of a gas' volume and pressure.

Bronchi: They are the branches of the trachea leading into the lungs.

Bronchial tree: It is the network of bronchi and bronchioles.

Bronchial-associated lymphatic tissue (BALT): It is the lymphoid tissue in the bronchial tree that helps fight germs.

Bronchioles: They are the branches of the bronchi leading into the pulmonary lobes.

Bronchitis: It is the inflammation of the bronchi and bronchioles leading to difficulty in breathing.

Bronchospasms: It is a sudden contraction of the bronchi or bronchioles in asthma or COPD.

Carbamino-haemoglobin: It is the haemoglobin chemically attached to carbon dioxide.

Coelom: It is the body cavity of invertebrates, filled with haemolymph.

Conchae: They are also called turbinates. They are the folds of the skull that swirl the air in your inner nose.

Conducting zone: It is the part of your respiratory system that takes air from the atmosphere to the lungs.

Congenital disease: It is a disease that happens to newborn babies, sometimes caught while still a foetus.

Diaphragm: It is a giant muscle attached to the ribs, sternum and spine that helps in breathing.

Emphysema: It is damage to lung tissue.

Epiglottis: A movable piece of cartilage that closes the wind pipe while swallowing food.

Eupnea: It means to breathe without making a conscious effort.

Goblet cells: They are the cells in the respiratory epithelium that make mucus.

Haemocyanin: It is the oxygen-carrier molecule in invertebrates.

Haemoglobin: It is the oxygen-carrier molecule in vertebrates.

Hilum: It is the point where bronchi, the pulmonary nerve and blood vessels enter the lungs.

Hyperpnea: It means to breathe with a conscious effort.

Hyperventilation: It means breathing very fast when worried or excited, till the person collapses.

Influenza: It is a disease of the respiratory system that causes cold and sneezing.

Intercostal muscles: They are the skeletal muscles between your ribs, used in breathing.

Lamina propria: It is the tissue covering the bronchi, which has BALT.

Laryngopharynx: It is the part of the pharynx above the larynx that acts as a resonating chamber.

Laryngospasm: It is a sudden closure of the larynx to stop fluid from entering the lungs.

Lingual tonsils: It is the lymphoid tissue under the tongue.

Meditation: It is an Asian method of calming the mind and body by breathing slowly and in a controlled manner.

Metastatic: This is a phase of cancer when the cancerous cells spread to other tissue.

Nasal-associated lymphoid tissue (NALT): It is the lymphoid tissue in the nose that helps fight germs.

Nasopharynx: It is the part of the pharynx between the nose and the mouth.

Operculum: It is the skin covering a fish's gills.

Oropharynx: It is the part of the pharynx where the food pipe and the wind pipe cross.

Oxyhaemoglobin: It is the haemoglobin that is chemically attached to oxygen.

Palatine tonsils: It is the lymphoid tissue in the oropharynx.

Pandemic: It is used to refer to a disease that spreads across the world.

Paranasal sinuses: They are the hollow, air-filled spaces in the skull that help clean air.

Partial pressure: It is the pressure exerted by a gas in a mixture of gases.

Pharyngeal tonsils: Also called adenoids, it is the lymphoid tissue in the nasopharynx.

Phlegm: It is the thick, germ-filled mucus that is coughed out.

Pleura: It is the bag that cushions the lungs.

Pollutant: It is anything in air or water that should not be there naturally.

Pulmonary arteries: They are the arteries that take deoxygenated blood from the heart to the lungs.

Pulmonary Function Test: It is a test that diagnoses lung condition by measuring how hard it is to breathe.

Pulmonary lobes: They are the internal divisions of the left and right lungs, further divided into segments, lobules and alveolar sacs.

Pulmonary oedema: It is a condition caused by plasma infiltrating the lungs.

Pulmonary surfactant: It is a soap-like liquid in the lungs that helps diffuse oxygen.

Pulmonary veins: They are the veins that take oxygenated blood from the lungs to the heart.

Pulmonary ventilation (PV): It is also called the respiratory cycle. It is a sequence of one inspiration and one expiration.

Respiratory bronchiole: It is the part of the bronchiole that ends in an alveolus.

Respiratory epithelium: It is the lining of the conducting zone of your respiratory system.

Respiratory zone: It is the part of your respiratory system that exchanges gases with blood.

Shock of life: It is the first breath taken by a newborn baby.

Trachea: It is the part of the respiratory system between the larynx and the lungs.

Trachealis muscle: It is the muscle that contracts the trachea.

Uvula: It is a flap of tissue that stops food going up into the inner nose.